PRAISE FOR *LEADING A*

"Generous churches don't just happen. They are the result of intentional focus on God's Word, a crystal-clear vision and a clean break from conventional wisdom that muzzles the generosity message. If you'll complete the daily readings and team exercises carefully crafted by Todd McMichen, I believe you'll unleash a generosity awakening right where you live and serve. Simple? -- Yes. Easy? -- Not likely. Profoundly powerful? -- Absolutely."

Larry Winger, CEO, Provision Ministry Group

"It is an honor to write on behalf of my former co-laborer in Christ -- Todd McMichen. He is 'one of the sharpest knives in the drawer' of my forty-four years of pastoral experience with staff ministers. His new book's blade cuts through much of the garbage-thinking and sell-out of so-called stewardship of the modern church. Todd is radically biblical, persistently practical, and refreshingly candid. I invite you to join his journey, not just to raise funds but to make real disciples of the Master."

Dr. Hayes Wicker, Senior Pastor, First Baptist Church in Naples, FL

"As a Pastor in my early 30s while leading a young, growing church, I am realizing how important the topic of generosity is to the process of discipleship, Todd McMichen has been a great teacher. This book provides wisdom from Proverbs along with concrete ways to best disciple people in their walks with Jesus. This is not a book solely about fundraising or giving; it is a book about discipleship and I have not been more challenged and encouraged personally, biblically or vocationally by anyone else like Todd regarding this topic. I highly recommend this book to Lead Pastors and lay leaders alike."

Riccardo Stewart, Lead Pastor, Redemption Church Tempe, AZ, and Team Chaplain for The Arizona State Football Team

"Todd McMichen is incapable of being uninteresting. When I get around him my hopes raise for my congregation and for the church universal. This guide through Proverbs will help you see that mine of wisdom in a new light—where its treasures for your thought and practice of stewardship will glimmer."

Dr. Jason Byassee, Senior Minister of Boone United Methodist Church in North Carolina, and research fellow in theology and leadership at Duke Divinity School

"Most church leaders do not get excited about a fund raising season, but they know no other path to fund the vision. Pastors have longed for another way to grow generosity that aligns to their discipleship passion. Todd McMichen provides a solid approach that will produce freedom, confidence, and engage your whole team."

Dr. Eric Geiger, Vice President, Resources Division, LifeWay Christian Resources and co-author of *Simple Church*

"Todd McMichen knows what it takes to grow generous disciples, and now through his writing, he's coaching you to do the exact same thing! Prepare to be challenged as you open the pages of this book full of real-life examples and practical exercises. The biblical principles Todd has applied through years of stewardship development in churches across the country are now available to you and me. I know your life, leadership, and ministry are going to be changed by his message."

Stuart Hodges, Lead Pastor, Waters Edge Church

"In *Leading a Generous Church*, Todd McMichen is true to form in taking us on a journey that results in our becoming more generous disciples. You can't read this book and not be impacted by the powerful truths, practical insights, and pointed challenges that come with each chapter. Get this book...read it... share it with your team...take your entire church through it...you won't regret it!"

David Putman, Lead Navigator with Auxano, conference leader, and co-author of *Breaking the Missional Code*

Todd McMichen

LEADING
A
generous
CHURCH

Making Disciples
without
Chasing Money

Leading a Generous Church:
Making Disciples without Chasing Money

Todd McMichen

© 2015 by Todd McMichen

Published by Rainer Publishing
www.rainerpublishing.com

ISBN 978-0692341292

Printed in the United States of America

To my parents, Bernie and Diana McMichen,
the most generous people I have ever met.

CONTENTS

ACKNOWLEDGEMENTS

To my family, Theresa, Riley, and Breanna, who have blessed me in that my generosity journey has been our generosity journey. Your willingness to support my travel while chasing my dream has encouraged scores of church leaders. You will never know how many times a pastor has thanked the Lord for your ministry and prayed for you while I have been on the road. How you model generosity in your own unique ways has continually inspired me and provided me with constant examples of how God uses each of us. Who would have thought standing as a young family in Naples, FL on a 100-acre future church site would result in a lifetime calling?

I would like to thank Will Mancini for his clarity insights, passion for discipleship, and systematic thinking which produced the book *Church Unique*. The Vision Frame is my obvious inspiration for growing a generous culture. To Jim Randall, who has pioneered, practiced, and provided great learning for me personally. To the Auxano team for their constant support and feedback, especially Andrea Kandler for reading, proofing, and double checking again and again.

ABOUT THE CHURCH UNIQUE
INTENTIONAL LEADER SERIES

The Series Originated Unexpectedly

Some things are found along the way, not calculated. Twelve years ago, my call into gospel ministry transitioned from pastoring in a local church to providing vision and strategy coaching for many churches. By God's grace I found unusual favor with a wide variety of pastors in different faith tribes and church models. I never planned to write, but eventually a passion for tool making would develop. Why? I observed firsthand how the right tool, at the right time, can change the trajectory of a church leader's calling. And it all started with the book *Church Unique*.

The Series is Not for Everyone

Please know that this series is not about minor improvements in your ministry. It's written with a higher aim—changed trajectory. Therefore, it carries a bold voice and challenging ideas. It's not written to make you feel good or to entertain. It's not an aggregation of good-idea blog posts. In fact, it's not really written for most church leaders. It's written for the hungry-to-learn leader, the passionate dreamer and the disciplined doer. It's written for the intentional few.

The Series is a Unique Collection

I grew up with a dad who worked non-stop around the house. He bought only Craftsman tools. I can remember the trademark red color of the Philips screwdrivers and the signature-shape of the chrome wrenches. The reason he bought Craftsman was the lifetime guarantee. The reason I liked them is they felt different in my hand.

So how will the Intentional Leader Series look and feel different? We aim for these features:

- **High transferability through model-transcendent principles.** We are not creating tools to guide the strategy or tactics of one approach. Most books do this even without explicitly acknowledging it. Every book is applicable to any ministry model.

- **Immediate usability on the front line of ministry.** The tools have been refined in real, messy ministry. We will prioritize the application for your leadership huddle or staff meeting next week.

- **Clarity-first conviction.** This series connects to the foundational work in *Church Unique*; and each book, while able to stand on its own, will relate to and reference the fundamental tools like the Kingdom Concept and Vision Frame. The books will relate more like engine gears than like distant cousins.

- **To-the-point style.** These aren't gift books or lite e-books created for advertising purposes. We want to bring short reads with sharp insight. We want a tool you can read in an hour, but change your leadership forever.

- **Gospel confidence.** The only real power center for ministry is the Gospel and we are not ashamed of this reality! (Romans 1:16) Therefore, no growth technique or creative innovation or smart idea should diminish a Gospel-centered outlook on ministry. This series will remind the reader that Jesus is sovereignly building His church (Matthew 16:18).

I hope you enjoy the contents of the series as we strive to bring you tools that are transferable, usable, integrated and direct. More than this, I hope they challenge your thinking and make you a better leader in your time and your place. Please stay in touch at WillMancini.com.

Will Mancini

INTRODUCTION

INTRODUCTION

Today is an amazing day to be leading Christ's church. In my 30 years of ministry I have never witnessed a more fruitful or engaging season. More and more churches are dreaming about God's unique vision. More and more churches are moving from a competitive mindset to a cooperative posture. Local and global missions are at the forefront of many congregations. Church planting and multi-campus strategies are flourishing. There is a resurgence of small church effectiveness in both urban and rural settings. I often tell pastors that if you are looking for an example or model from which to learn, you can find at least one church that has already done exactly what you are thinking of doing.

When I began my journey in ministry this was not the case. Every church pretty much looked the same, had the same programming schedule, sang the same songs, and even had the same dress code. Churches were more likely to compete with each other and were largely non-supportive of para-church organizations. I believe we're beginning to see changes for the better. Now, you may feel trapped in a church of the past. Or you may feel constrained in a congregation that seriously lacks forward momentum. The good news is today you have options. You do not have to be like the church down the street to succeed. However, you do need to know your specific mission and learn to channel your resources toward it.

One of the most inspiring transitions that I have watched the modern church explore and begin to prioritize is in the area of generosity. The church money crisis hit mainstream back in the 1980s when several high profile ministries were rocked with financial scandals. I don't want to throw stones, but in order to give a little flavor to the real life money messages being transmitted, here are a couple of nuggets from the past. You could have turned on your television and witnessed a praying Jerry Falwell in his Sunday suit careening down a water slide to raise $1,000,000 for a fallen PTL empire. At the time the total fund raising bail out exceeded $22,000,000. If you missed that, then Oral Roberts was held up in the top of a prayer tower for the final stages of his $8,000,000 funding crisis. He even stated that God told him he would "be called home" if the funds didn't come through from supporters. When the mainstream media picked up these stunts and ran them for months, the negative effects stuck for years.

It led to a period of silence in the church about money. No pastor wanted to talk about it. So, a new dialogue became common vernacular when the offering plate was passed. "This offering is not for our guests to participate in. It is only for our members, so guests let it pass you by." These little statements also unintentionally erased the power of generosity and the need for discipleship from church programming.

However, money forced its way back to the forefront in 2008 with the financial crisis in America. This crisis resulted in the personal pain of many individuals and ministries. Church leaders had to learn how to comfort the hurting while sharing dwindling resources. Church leaders were forced to rethink their vision and model. A big question surfaced: "How do we continue to impact lives with limited resources?" New dreams were birthed that adjusted staff structure, ministry alignment, and resource allocation. This new day also called church leaders to re-engage in a public conversation about finances and the word "generosity" became the buzz word.

This newfound need resulted in the dramatic growth of helpful organizations like Dave Ramsey's Financial Peace University, which has become a common place tool in the local church. However, most church leaders are still uncomfortable with the money conversation. They are glad to have someone teach a class or hire a professional to create the challenge, but would have little confidence that they could unleash a revolution of generosity within their church.

I have been highly invested as both a staff member and stewardship consultant for 30 years. I have seen the days when growth and money flowed easily, as well as the opposite. I can assure you there is definitely a pattern to churches who continually experience the highest levels of generosity. It doesn't have to do with being a large church, in a growing area, with a high percentage of above average wage earners raised in the Bible belt. The most consistent factor is the senior pastor and staff leadership. For this reason, I wanted to prepare a guide and help a church staff increase their confidence as passionate stewardship leaders that know how to grow generous disciples.

Several years ago I was teaching a series at my church through the Book of Proverbs and began to notice that every single chapter contained multiple passages of financial wisdom. This guide will call you to read a proverb a day. I am asking you to note every scripture that teaches you something about resources. You will notice that we are to pursue wisdom as if it was a precious resource like gold or silver. There will be practical advice about storing up resources little by little like an ant. You will be challenged in both your work ethic and generosity levels. I will highlight one principle from each chapter, but do not let your learning be limited to my thoughts. At the end of each week you will be provided with a *Staff Team Up* to engage in a collaborative discussion delivering measurable results to help your team become passionate and effective stewardship leaders.

Proverbs 1:1-2 sets the tone well: "*The proverbs of Solomon son of David, king of Israel: for gaining wisdom and instruction; for understanding words of insight.*" This book is written for you and your team to gain wisdom, understanding, and insight. So let the journey begin.

Remember you have three simple instructions:

- Read a proverb a day, taking note of all wisdom that can be related to resources.

- Read and reflect upon the passages I provide.

- Fully participate in the weekly *Staff Team Up*.

THINKING LIKE A DISCIPLE CHASER

THINKING LIKE A DISCIPLE CHASER

Whenever I speak on the topic of creating a generous culture, I almost always begin with the following illustration. I want you to imagine a staircase that has ten steps toward a second floor level. On the first floor is a first-time guest that is considering attending your church. Up on the second floor is a mature, generous disciple. Now, if you were to create a journey that led this first time guest up the stairs toward becoming a fully mature, generous disciple, what experiences would he or she need to have on each growth step? What would they need to learn, see, or feel? Who would they need to meet? Where would they need to be engaged? What disciplines would they need to acquire? What freedoms and passions would need to be unleashed? How many years might this journey take to move from a first time guest to a generous disciple?

Take the time to think about the information, truths, and stories that a person would need to experience. Then record these, one on each step.

Once you have completed your 10-step growth track, take the time to make a list of the different ministries that you would need to engage to carry out your plan. Because once you know the ministry list, you will need to prepare materials, a ministry calendar, and do some training. If your process takes more or less than 10 steps, that is fine too.

Once you have completed these two lists, one of experiences and the other of ministries, what surprises you about your work?

I know your track is probably unique. But every time I do this exercise, invariably the first step has something to do with a positive first visit. This step might involve ministries like the Parking Lot Team, Greeter Team, Preschool Team, plus several others. When was the last time your staff gave consideration to how a generous culture begins in the parking lot? How does this change the way we think about growing generous disciples?

Now I want you to think of a different scenario. Imagine your church has set forth a faith-based budget for the year that resulted in a challenging financial growth number. It is early in the year, so growth has yet to meet expectations and financial pressure is beginning to rise. The pastor calls a staff meeting and gives the floor to the financial administrator. He or she describes the situation in guarded terms because it feels like poor leadership, but no one is brave enough to say it. The remedy is then announced. The pastor is going to send out a letter before summer for a catch up offering so the church does not dig deeper in a hole with camps and mission trips that are planned. Everyone is to watch the thermostats and light switches around the facility. A ministry spending freeze is also enacted. The meeting ends with an awkward silence and the side bar conversations begin.

Which staff meeting would you rather be a part of? The one which creates a generous culture in advance from the parking lot forward, or the one in which your ministry skills are reduced to being a switch flipper?

It is interesting to me that if I was to ask a worship leader how to take a first-time guest and grow them into a powerfully contributing member somewhere in the worship ministry, that growth track would be second nature. However, when it comes to the topic of money we feel uncertain. It is as simple and freeing as training a new greeter or small group leader. You just need to know your path. We begin this path forward in Proverbs.

WEEK 1:
YOU CHASE
WHAT YOU VALUE

WEEK 1

YOU CHASE WHAT YOU VALUE

YOUNG CHURCH, USA

This church is led by a young man who has gone to a church growth conference, and was told to not talk about money because it will chase people away. He was also formerly the youth pastor on staff in the local First Church in which the finance committee locked down resources like Fort Knox. This taught him not to trust a lay person to have influence over money. At this point he has never pastored a church, formed a budget, hired a staff, or led an organization through the ups and downs of a fiscal cycle. Yet, he is geared not to talk about resources or to lean on the business leaders in his church for help.

Things go well for a while, but the pressure begins to surface. Staff was hired prematurely because he heard, at the same conference incidentally, that you hire staff in advance of growth. Only the growth didn't materialize as projected. In truth, the young church is growing fine. However, it doesn't feel like it because expenses and giving are not in sync.

How do you talk about money now, in a place where you have never talked about it before or structured yourself for support? At first, he tries to solve the problem himself which leads to stress on his home and staff. Then he begins to broach the subject with his leaders in a lighthearted fashion to not be alarming. One who understands the value of money and leading well quickly calls him out. The pastor began his ministry chasing a culture free of the negative money conversation. In the end, he created the very thing he was running from.

The one thing he has done well is enlist competent leaders. Their lives have been changed along with those of their friends. The passion they have for their church is unquestioned. They quickly realize he is in a little over his head. So they jump to his support. A plan is developed to sharpen their pencils on non-growth oriented expenses. One leader offers to speak to the congregation about all that God is doing and how they have to all step up together. Then three leaders offer to make significant one time gifts while going to others for the same response. This creativity, ownership, and confidence both relieves and inspires the young pastor. He did not know nor had he ever experienced a healthy generosity culture. Now, he is on the journey.

PROVERBS 1 - WHERE YOUR TREASURE IS

*"Such are the paths of all who go after **ill-gotten gain**; it takes away the life of those who get it." (Proverbs 1:19 NIV)*

The topics of money and enjoyment of life go hand-in-hand far too often. Life is a journey, a continual path to a preferred destination. Most are pursuing a better life unless they have become frustrated by the obstacles along the way and quit. Your perceived prize at the end of the journey is determined by your heart's eyes at the beginning of the journey. It will be so disheartening to get to the end and realize your heart was skewed to gain the wrong prize, and your life is now gone.

You can't stop the heart. It is the seat of your passions, both good and bad. When you were a teenager your heart fell in love. This young love motivated so many actions, like sweaty palms, loss of appetite, a mind consumed, and even a willingness to deceive your parents. The heart is still the most powerful influence of your actions as an adult. If you are passionate about college football it can cause you to prioritize your time, reading materials, conversations, and resources. If you are passionate about shopping, exercise, or the outdoors, your life will be influenced accordingly.

If you want to lead a generous church, the senior leadership must become passionate about generosity. Your heart must be overcome. Stewardship must become a driving force shaping your culture. Be mindful that a generous culture produces many results beyond a surplus of finances. It helps with volunteerism, impact in society, personal faith, and a more positive disposition. I have never met an unhappy, over-stressed, or weary obedient steward. Who doesn't want these positive characteristics to permeate church culture?

Often when churches pursue generosity, they pursue more money. The pursuit of money is not the same as producing a generous disciple. Money can be gained quickly, but the strategy can contain unintended negative results. If the ill-gotten gain is money, the proper gain must be a transformed disciple. And that transformed disciple may need to begin with you.

Take Away: On a scale of 1-10 (with 1 being low and 10 being high), where would you rate your stewardship passion?

PROVERBS 2 - CHASING SUCCESS

*"He holds **success** in store for the upright, he is a shield to those whose walk is blameless." (Proverbs 2:7 NIV)*

Everyone wants to be successful with life. However, success can be measured and pursued many different ways. For some, to be successful has a strong reliance on the accumulation of resources. For others, a standard of personal success is acquired by some level of social acceptance. Still others see the recreational lifestyles of peers and begin chasing it for themselves.

It has been a repeated experience of mine in ministry to watch a young church move from a portable facility to a permanent facility. It would not be unusual for this to result in extremely dramatic growth. The preaching is the same, the worship is the same, and even the level of personal integrity is the same. However, the appearance of greater external success is clearly different. Then, when the church growth slows it is easy for the staff to second guess themselves. My question is always, who is responsible for the success? We take far too much of the credit for the climb.

God created you in this place and time. He caused you to be born into a family, community, and granted you many unique experiences. He has equipped you with gifts, skills, abilities, and relationships. He has a specific mission for you to accomplish. He alone has created you to be successful and holds your success in His hand. Think about that for a minute. You are created, called, equipped, and guaranteed success by your almighty caring Father. A failure at success for your life is only possible if you lack one thing: The passionate pursuit of it as if it was your most valuable asset achievement.

*"Indeed, if you call out for insight and cry aloud for understanding, and if you look for it as for **silver** and search for it as for **hidden treasure**." (Proverbs 2:3, 4 NIV)*

A proper definition of personal success both in your finances and career is important. Become aware of both the inner tendency for false measurement and the fearful embrace of external pressure. Seek God's determined plan of success for you. Where might you find it? Here is a hint: Look in His right hand.

Take Away: How does it make you feel knowing that God has your life success in His hand?

PROVERBS 3 - GOD OWNS EVERYTHING

*"Honor the Lord with your **wealth**, with the **first fruits** of all your crops; then your barns will be filled to overflowing, and your vats will brim over with new wine." (Proverbs 3:9,10 NIV)*

Stewardship success is 100% impossible without embracing this valued principle: God owns everything. We are stewards of a small few things that God owns. God owns my life, my salvation, my uniqueness, my calling, my family, my job, my church, my body, my car, my bank account, my cash, and my television.

We are asked to give God the first of everything. This is a position of your heart that creates habits for our hands, which grows a pathway for your life journey. Financial stress stems from the belief that we own our resources, which means we deserve the right for more and are responsible for the pressure to deliver. It inherently creates a tightened fist with sleepless nights rather than a generous, open hand.

It is God's responsibility to provide for you, your church and family, not your responsibility. Your responsibility is to release ownership and be an obedient steward. This is why I believe the inherent values related to tithing are critical for growth. Values like surrender, trust, faith, and fruitfulness. Now I know that whether or not a tithe is still considered a biblical command to be practiced today is widely debated. Nevertheless, my conviction is that it is a great life practice, and I honestly hope you tithe. However, this book is not about tithing, but generosity. The goal is not to get you or your entire church to tithe (but I bet you would take it if it occurred). My goal is to get you to release the ownership of your resources and grow toward a lifestyle of giving away far more than 10% of your income, while influencing others to follow in your footsteps.

As a lead discipler you need to go first. Release ownership and become a humble, faithful steward.

<u>Take Away:</u> Write out a personal deed of ownership thanking God and granting Him authority over every resource in your life.

PROVERBS 4 - WHAT'S IT REALLY WORTH?

*"The beginning of wisdom is this: Get wisdom. Though it **cost** all you have, get understanding." (Proverbs 4:7 NIV)*

I grew up in a blue collar family. My dad was one of those men that took a shower after work, not before. The smell of his work clothes was something that truly astounded me as a kid. Now, I had some good fortune, our home happened to be located in a more affluent side of town. It was formerly owned by my mom's grandmother, and we purchased it from her estate. I can remember being so shocked when I heard my friends talk about me as if my family was rich. My parents weren't rich, but they were wise and generous. Money can't solve every problem, but wisdom can. Get wisdom, not money.

We try to use wisdom to evaluate expenses based on their cost. Is this product or service worth the price I am going to pay to receive the expected result? We make the purchase if the price is right. Sometimes we make the mistake of purchasing even if the price isn't right.

Have you ever noticed the cost of an expense beyond the dollar amount? Typically, we are wise enough to read the fine print even on items that are being advertised as "free." Everything has a cost. Financial wisdom or a lack of it can affect many areas of your life (v. 13, 22). It can impact your future rewards, experiences, and opportunities (v. 8-9). It can impact your physical choices, like sleep and food (v. 16-17). Lack of wisdom can certainly affect you spiritually and emotionally (v. 23).

I see this all of the time in churches. We hold on to unproductive expenses, because we do not want to face the ministry leader who has had ownership for the past decade. Or we fall in love with the cheapest builder down the road who promises the moon only to discover he often over-promises and under-delivers. It is not about the amount of money involved. It is about financial wisdom. What does it truly cost you to do the wrong thing with money?

God's Word is full of life wisdom, and your finances are connected to every area of your life. Your well of financial wisdom impacts your day through many different experiences. While money can cover a lot of pains, just remember what happens when money is tight. We can become anxious, worrisome, impatient, and even angry. Chase God's wisdom though it costs you everything.

Take Away: What if the only financial wisdom your people ever received came from your church? What would they know? How much life help and discipleship are you providing?

PROVERBS 5 - MONEY IS POWERFUL

*"Lest strangers feast on your **wealth** and your toil enrich the house of another." (Proverbs 5:10 NIV)*

Money is one of the most influential forces in our world. It has been used to create the appearance of security and success. It both empowers and impoverishes people. It can even boost your self-esteem and give you a fun rush. Who doesn't love pay day or a new outfit or great vacations? Money influences how we experience and evaluate our lives.

This passage is about the power of a tempting experience. A young man can become wise by listening to his father, teacher, and other mentors. However, when you are young it is difficult to know your limitations. Temptation is so easy to follow. Then it leads to a path of destruction which robs you of life.

We are easily tempted every day to chase the wrong thing. Money is a gift from God to provide for our families, allow us to experience some personal pleasure, and to extend His love to others through generosity. But just like everything else this gift of grace can be turned into a powerful deceiver (v. 3). I promise you that we all have areas of constant temptation related to money and possessions. When I was younger I was so jealous of people who had more. I wanted what they had, because it looked fun and better than what I possessed. When I did not have it, it caused me to feel discouraged.

This is just one small example. We are all tempted each week to solve emotional, physical, and spiritual problems with money. In the end this drive can rob us of life (v. 10-11). Life is full of stages, sometimes we have more, then sometimes we have less. Money is simply a gift in our lives. It is not the foundation of our ability to survive or succeed. You can be poor and be happy. You can have tremendous influence and impact with minimal financial resources. I witness smaller churches all of the time having exponential impact. While I also see well-resourced congregations weighed down by a lack of financial wisdom.

Do not chase money, but chase disciples. Do not limit your vision or become a slave to your finances. Money is just one of the many resources God provides you to meet your needs and fulfill His purpose.

Take Away: Make a list of all the resources you have at your disposal. Does your ministry strategy wisely channel all these resources at their most productive level?

PROVERBS 6 - PATHS TO MORE MONEY

*"A little **sleep**, a little **slumber**, a little folding of the hands to **rest**—"* (Proverbs 6:10 NIV)

There is pretty much a universal desire in all of us for more money. I am not sure there is anything inherently wrong with that. When I speak to business leaders I consistently exhort them to not be afraid to earn as much money as possible for the goal of giving as much away as possible. However, when church leaders desire more money, they often only know one way to achieve the goal. It is to get people to give more money.

The Bible actually describes different paths that cause money to exchange hands. Generous churches understand these paths and are striving to apply God's wisdom in all areas. Here they are in Proverbs.

- Money exchanges hands to fulfill a debt. (v. 1)

- Money is possessed in savings or reserves. (v. 6-8)

- Money is distributed for work completed. (v. 10-11)

- Money is released through spending on expenses. (v. 30-31)

Here is the good news. If you want to increase the financial resources at your church, let's say you have four buckets. Here is the challenge. You also have four areas that require obedience and wisdom. Spending less is not the same as spending wisely. Continually asking for more is not the same as growing a generous culture. For-profit businesses fight waste, constantly measure return on investment, and would never be satisfied with spending more than they receive every year. As church leaders we can learn a lot from God's Word and the marketplace.

My experience is that most church staff do not experience common ownership for comprehensive financial responsibility in the church. It can begin when a staff member submits an annual ministry budget request for more than is needed, knowing that a lower number will probably be approved. There is always the guy who can't keep up with his expenses to budget or the gal who thinks her ministry is more important than someone else's ministry. Of course the pastor's job is to preach more on money, bearing the fund raising load alone. The administrator should keep expenses in line. There can be many individual silos and so little focused energies. Remember, it takes a team of leaders and stewards with a comprehensive strategy to grow a generous church.

Take Away: How would your people describe the financial climate of your church as an organization?

PROVERBS 7 - MISLEADING PEOPLE IS ALWAYS POSSIBLE

*"Today I fulfilled my vows, and I have food from my **fellowship offering** at home." (Proverbs 7:14 NIV)*

This proverb is actually a statement of deception, an enticement to do wrong in the name of good. While no leader ever looks forward to realizing that poor leadership has occurred, he would be foolish to ignore reality.

Since my kids were old enough to understand, I have repeated a small pearl of wisdom: "It is easier to blame than to be responsible." I confess, I still struggle surrendering to this one. So maybe you and I are together on this.

It is rare that I encounter a church leader who readily admits to embracing a leadership lifestyle that lacks wisdom. After all, who wants to go around promoting they are a "fool." Nevertheless, we have to be authentic with the past before we can make wise decisions in the present with the hope of future rewards.

Sometimes leaders make honest mistakes with money. Other times we actually sin with it. When we have realized disobedience, if we allow it to linger, we are digging a deep hole. I would like to end the week providing you an opportunity to confess any financial failings as a leader. I would also like for you to consider what confession you may need to make on behalf of your people. There is biblical precedent for this; just think of the time the children of Israel and their leaders wrongly used their resources creating the golden calf. Moses did some serious praying, then God restored the promise of a blessed future.

Take Away: Record a prayer of confession and surrender. Receive God's grace and a promised future. Review the *Staff Team Up* and come prepared to add value to your team.

STAFF TEAM UP

Set aside two to three hours and come prepared to collaborate as a team. You will need a flip chart and markers for these exercises.

Each staff member should take a turn and share three lessons learned this week.

- What did you learn and apply from the devotions in Proverbs this week?

- What insights did you gain that can be applied to your ministry or church?

- What verse did you find on your own in Proverbs or elsewhere in Scripture that has a stewardship principle or implication?

Create a list of three to five core values that will serve to guide your team as the designated stewardship leaders moving forward. Consider the following areas:

- A value related to staff/church leaders being wise, responsible, and growing as personal stewardship leaders.

- A value related to the priority of discipling all ages toward a generous Christian.

- A value related to church budget, spending, and generosity.

- A value related to celebrating generosity.

- A value toward accountability and process.

To support these values, create statements providing both a definition of what is meant as well as multiple examples of how and where they will be applied. Consider letting the examples begin with "demonstrated by..." Each value may have two to three "demonstrated by" expressions.

To anchor these new stewardship values, locate one to three Scripture verses for each value, which will provide further encouragement, discipleship, and direction.

Illustration: *"Start Life-Giving Conversations"*

We are passionate about the power of positive conversations. Our words come from our heart and the generous heart of God will be loud.

- *Demonstrated by telling stories at leadership meetings of how life change is occurring in ministry areas due to the positive generosity of our people.*

- *Demonstrated by expressing thankfulness in our worship services for the abundant generosity we have received both from God our provider and our people on a weekly basis.*

- *Demonstrated by personally thanking volunteers and investors one on one.*

The tongue has the power of life and death, and those who love it will eat its fruit. (Proverbs 18:21 NIV)

And they exceeded our expectations: They gave themselves first of all to the Lord, and then by the will of God also to us. (2 Corinthians 8:5 NIV)

For you know the grace of our Lord Jesus Christ, that though he was rich, yet for your sake he became poor, so that you through his poverty might become rich. (2 Corinthians 8:9 NIV)

WHY THIS EXERCISE IS IMPORTANT:

Language is one of the most important tools you have as a leader. With language you direct, inspire, inform, and communicate. Clear communication and modeling are actually the two most basic activities in a leadership relationship. You show; you instruct.

Pastors tend to lack confidence, because they do not have a defined language that arises naturally from their hearts. Do you remember how awkward it sounded when you took a foreign language class in school? I took years of Spanish and never was able to sound confident and passionate when I conversed.

Clearly stating agreed upon values in your own words that are grounded in the Scriptures that you select is empowering. When you are in a collaborative environment and your team creates values that impact all ministries, it will provide both accountability and direction for your team. Everyone should see their role and be inspired to create their strategy in the future.

Be sure to have fun and be creative. Let your uniqueness inform your expression. The process is just as important as the product. Do not rush to get to the end result. Feel free to be memorable, inspiring, and actionable. Some churches lean toward creating catchy slogans, while others lean toward biblical language. There is no right or wrong. Just be yourself.

WEEK 2:
YOU MEASURE
WHAT MATTERS

WEEK 2

YOU MEASURE WHAT MATTERS

ESTABLISHED CHURCH, USA

The mature church with a tenured pastor can have both disadvantages and advantages over the younger churches. The disadvantages can include a history that binds and a decision-making process that constricts. It can be challenged by long-standing loyalties that may have seen better days and an older facility that is costly to maintain. On the other hand, a long tenured pastor who has built a healthy, sustainable, and flexible culture possesses an enviable resource. Maturity definitely has its advantages.

The mature pastor has seen good times come and go. He should be less reactionary to the challenges of the moment and more faithfully responsive to the objectives of the future. He knows things ebb and flow, that momentum can go up and down. The ability not to panic and not start pushing buttons is a gift to his staff.

Longevity in ministry should produce a clear vision that enjoys deep roots. Over time the right leaders should be in place having been trained to do things the right way without needing to be micromanaged. These trained leaders should exist in systems that are well-maintained and run smoothly. All should be enjoying the process of watching disciples and ministries producing inspiring results. Focus, alignment, and repetition over time win!

Another benefit is the depth of relationships. Studies show that the most generous gifts are consistently received by non-profits with a long-time senior leader. The committed investment to the organization and into the lives of those it benefits reaps both trust and support. It becomes much easier to talk about what is most important. You know whom to approach about what based on their experience and passions. A friend talking to a friend is so much easier than raising money from a stranger.

Of course, I am repeatedly surprised by the long-tenured pastor in the established church who sees all the problems, but is blind to his own responsibilities. If you plant good seed, in good soil, and care for it, great stuff happens. It may take years, but it shouldn't take decades.

Disciples are not grown only in a class or through a sermon series. They also result from time and from relationships that are seasoned by purposeful conversations.

PROVERBS 8 - IT'S TIME TO GROW

*"With me are **riches** and honor, enduring **wealth** and **prosperity**."*
(Proverbs 8:18 NIV)

It is not uncommon for people to divide their lives into sections. We have our work lives and home lives. Our spiritual lives and physical lives. We can get even further compartmentalized when we have our public spiritual lives and our private spiritual lives. Then, we have areas of our life that we allow our faith to impact and others that we would never let our faith touch. For instance, many Christians can view their money as separate from their faith. It gets even worse when we view money as having no faith value or as something of the world.

This proverb is clear. Inside God's wisdom are resources that He wants to bless us with. He realizes that we have a drive for more resources and wants to redirect the flame (v. 10-11, 19-21). The problem isn't that money is evil, but that loving money outside of obedient discipleship is evil. The pursuit should be for wisdom and maturity, not the resources.

At "Numbers Church" you know what the measuring stick is. It is how many people were here this weekend, how much money was collected, and how many new members they can report. These numbers are not necessarily wrong to measure. They do provide some helpfulness in planning. However, they are not the true marks of discipleship. Churches struggle with discovering how to measure what a disciple is and where they are maturing. As leaders of the church we have to move beyond this struggle. If we cannot quantify discipleship, then how will we know if we are succeeding? I know what you might be thinking, "You can't measure the heart." Correct, but we can create some tools that lead people toward discerning personal fruitfulness.

We all need to grow as passionate, obedient disciples. Most struggle with an accurate discernment of their progress. If we only have false ways to measure, then the answers will be untrue. The measurement is in chasing wisdom. If you run after the right goal, good things will follow.

This pursuit of wisdom will cause us to understand God's plan for our lives and our resources. It will also produce both physical and eternal fruit that is beyond human explanation. So, you need to grow in your discipleship, then you must prioritize the discipleship of the people God has entrusted you to lead well.

Take Away: Create a list of at least 10 personal life priorities or habits you would expect to find in a generous disciple. These should be tangible expressions of a personal faith that you should be able to disciple toward.

PROVERBS 9 - TIPPERS AND NON-GIVERS

*"**Stolen** water is sweet; food eaten in secret is delicious!" (Proverbs 9:17 NIV)*

Wisdom reveals; it does not hide. Only a fool believes that wrong things enjoyed in private do not matter. Now giving is not a matter to be boasted about. However, being in denial over the state of our heart—and that of our people—is foolish.

Early on in my ministry, I naively thought that most people gave and even tithed. It was how I was raised. I have pretty much always tithed and been involved in campaigns dating back to the 1980s when I was a teenager. I found myself diving into the real facts as I became more involved in the finances and stewardship of the church. It is not over-stating the case that many times 20% of the people do 80% of the giving. Now this is not always accurate, but you would be shocked by how your numbers shake out. Even more shocking are the times when pastors and staff are not giving and tithing. Can you imagine what your church would be like if more passionate stewards were engaged? It will never happen until we lead it to happen.

Let's start with why people occasionally tip God or give Him nothing instead of being generous. Here are some reasons that you might consider:

- They do not trust the church

- They are poor or struggling

- They do not know how to participate

- They are hurting or in crisis

- They are mad at church leadership

- They have never been led well

- They are poor money managers

- They don't understand how the church functions together

- They do not know what it would be used for

- They have never seen a positive effect of a church donation

- They have never heard generosity celebrated

- They are selfish

- They are worrisome and lack trust

- They simply do not know they should

All of these issues and many others can be solved by grace and discipleship. But, you do not know how to create a strategy when the problem is not being honestly revealed. The easiest solution is to call people out or just give up because the mountain is too daunting. First, make sure you are a generous leader so you can be followed. Then, see tippers and non-givers through eyes of grace that need to be discipled for their benefit and not church financial gain.

Take Away: Create your own list regarding why you believe people in your ministry are less generous than they should be.

PROVERBS 10 - OBEDIENT AND EXTRAVAGANT GIVERS

*"The Lord does not let the righteous go **hungry**, but he thwarts the **craving** of the wicked." (Proverbs 10:3 NIV)*

A tiny portion of people in your church are consistently obedient givers. I would place these types of people in two categories: those who tithe and those who give beyond their tithe. Some of these may actually have the gift of giving while others are well-trained disciples.

When I was a teenager my parents taught me to work, save, and tithe. Also during this time my home church was in the midst of a capital campaign and asked me to give above and beyond my tithe for three years to help finance the building of the new worship center. I am so grateful for my parents who trained me and my church which invited me into the generous life.

For those who work hard, spend wisely, and live the generous life, God promises to continue to provide. You will not go hungry (vs. 3), and He will multiply your resources (vs. 4-5). Time and time again I have witnessed both the miraculous and extravagant provisions of God. I hope you have done the same. Speaking honestly, I can't remember a time in my wage-earning life when I did not consistently tithe, nor have I ever experienced God not coming through for me. I have had to do without the nicest of vacations, cars, clothes, and toys. My kids have not had the best of the best. I have lost my job, been unemployed, wondered how to pay my rent, and struggled with what the next meal would be. I have also been blessed to golf some great courses, travel in first class, and give away more than I ever dreamed.

Giving is a testimony of God's grace in your life. It affirms your faith and how God desires to work in the world. You are declaring your faith again every time you give. When you then give extravagantly, you are truly participating at a high level in the advancement of the gospel mission. You truly understand what is important to God, how He works in the world and desires to partner with you.

The gospel, the grace, and the love of God is nothing less than an extravagant gift. He came not to be served, but to give His life as a ransom for many. Take the time to celebrate generosity today as a means of sharing the gospel.

Take Away: I hope you noticed the stewardship gems in verses 2-5, 14-16, and 20-22. Part of becoming a passionate steward is putting up your antenna to how God's Word constantly discusses your resources. There are even a few other verses in this proverb that provide wisdom to your resources. Can you locate them?

PROVERBS 11 - IMPACTING YOUR CITY

*"When the righteous **prosper**, the city rejoices; when the wicked perish, there are shouts of joy. Through the **blessing of the upright** a city is exalted, but by the mouth of the wicked it is destroyed." (Proverbs 11:10, 11 NIV)*

This verse is a powerful confirmation of how discipleship results in impact. When one is growing in righteousness, their life has a positive impact on society. When one is growing in righteousness, the blessings flow onto the city. So what comes first—discipleship, outreach, or generosity? Both church outreach and generosity are the result of a life that is being discipled toward righteous living. One of the disciplines of righteous living is not only financial generosity to the church, but generous living in society. Neighborhoods, schools, marketplaces, parks, and civic activities invite the righteous to participate generously.

God calls His people to impact its city. Which means God is calling your church to impact your city. In the past, churches were largely concerned with keeping their members, funding their programs, and protecting their capital investments. However, there has been a strong growing trend to serve our cities. Our eyes were first opened during the events of 9/11, then later with Hurricane Katrina, and finally the economic disaster of 2008. In between each of these events we had some of the most devastating tornadoes, fires, floods, and hurricanes specific areas of our country have ever experienced.

These dramatic needs catalyzed what is now becoming more common through our churches—organized and collaborative city serve events that are sweeping across the country. As a matter of fact, community outreach is quickly becoming one of the easiest ways to connect with your city and engage the community. Often new guests to your church will more easily jump into a service project before committing to membership or a small group.

Generosity is not just a growing trend, but it is now an integral part of corporate and popular culture. If you and your church are not actively collaborating with other organizations and strategically serving your city, then you are quickly falling behind. God expects His church to lead the way in terms of generosity and city engagement. This means you have to organize vision, leadership, ministries, and finances to be externally-driven. A great question to ask is, "What is our community saying about our church?" Is it a facility or programming complement? Better yet, is it a serving-our-city compliment?

Take Away: Where do you volunteer and give outside the church for society impact?

PROVERBS 12 - BECOMING A GENEROUS LEADER

*"Those who **work** their land will have abundant food, but those who chase fantasies have no sense." (Proverbs 12:11 NIV)*

This may either be surprising or offensive to you. A common conclusion among many lay people is that pastors are not hard workers. When I hear them speak in these terms it is not the usual joke about only working one day a week, but a serious concern regarding the work ethic of pastors. Now I know a lot of pastors that work long hours and are devoted to their profession. However, I have also met several who struggle.

This chapter repeatedly addresses the calling to work hard. It further states that God blesses those who do so (vs. 11, 14, 24, and 27). Throughout my ministry I made sure that I gave my church at least a full work week. Additionally, I volunteered both in my own church and in my community. Give this some thought, high capacity lay people work hard in the marketplace, volunteer to make an impact in their community, and serve in the leadership of their local church.

As a matter of fact, this is probably what every pastor preaches that great lay people do. Are you providing the example of a generous lifestyle? Work hard, find a place of meaningful volunteerism in your church, and do the same in your community. Your vocation should not become a reason you serve less than others. Lead the way.

The most fruitful run in my life was when I worked full-time as a consultant, volunteered to serve as a pastor in a church, and volunteered as the chaplain for the local public high school. While I simply did it out of passion and calling, this platform was such a challenge to men in my church and community to live a generous life of great impact. Chase discipleship not resources.

Take Away: If you were to resign your job and take employment outside the church, what would you willingly volunteer to do as your ministry? Create your own job description based on your passion, gifts, and vision. Evaluate your weekly efforts to see how this exercise needs to inform your current day-to-day priorities.

PROVERBS 13 - MEASURING SUCCESS

*"One person pretends to be **rich**, yet has nothing; another pretends to be **poor**, yet has great **wealth**." (Proverbs 13:7 NIV)*

It is easy to fake success. Credit cards and car leases have certainly made the appearance of financial success more readily available on a personal level. Several years ago I read that one leading high-end foreign automaker leased 90% of their cars currently driven in America. No one can afford to buy one, so the cars are leased.

In church-world, success is often measured in comparison to the hottest author or speaker's church. It is easy enough to have a cool logo, popular mission statement, current website, dress trendy, and have a social media following. However, how will we measure true success? God's Word is clear. We are called to glorify Him and make disciples. Part of disciple making is generosity.

Honest conversations in practical terms are absolutely necessary to discern true success. Regularly when I show up to work with a client I start the meeting by requesting an update on progress. I usually get responses like "Sunday was good" or "everything feels real positive" or "no negative comments are surfacing." Then you have the professional nay-sayer who can bring momentum to a screeching halt just by mentioning some concerns he has related to timing and feel. Nothing quantitative, but a powerfully subjective opinion controlling forward progress.

It is important to know what you are measuring. Write it down so that the measurement is the standard and not our perception of the process. Faking success can produce temporary peace. Injecting cautionary subjective opinion can be alarming. The truth sets people free to give.

There is no shortcut or quick, easy path to a generous church. It is one little decision after another after another (vs. 11, 18, 22). When churches avoid an honest money conversation they inevitably are headed down the wrong path and have little hope of growing generous disciples.

However, when you lead one small decision at a time with the ultimate goal of growing a generous culture, even the most uncomfortable of conversations can become acceptable. Here are a series of small decisions you can begin to make to learn to measure how you are doing.

Are you:

- Talking about generosity weekly in your staff meetings?

- Regularly celebrating generosity in worship?

- Setting aside at least 10% of church donations to give away?

- Spending less than you are receiving, so you can be prepared to say "yes" to God's surprise opportunities?

- Regularly praying for people to be blessed at work?

- Regularly praying for those who are struggling?

- Publicly and personally thanking people for their generosity?

- Regularly showing people what impact their generosity is having?

- Constantly evaluating your expenses and financial processes?

- Having multiple training opportunities for the least to the most generous?

- These are just a few thoughts, why not create a list that is more personal to your church and ministry?

<u>Take Away:</u> Create a list of honest questions that will remind you to build a generous culture in your ministry. Remember to contextualize it to your current area of responsibility.

PROVERBS 14 - WHAT IF?

*"All hard work brings a **profit**, but mere talk leads only to **poverty**." (Proverbs 14:23 NIV)*

I love the experience of being rewarded whether it is pay day, a gift at my birthday, a great shot on the golf course, or a hard fought victory by my favorite athletic team. Rewards are affirming, fun, and energizing.

This proverb is all about God's rewards for obedient stewardship. In verse one we will be rewarded for the labor of our hands. Hard work is rewarded with an abundant harvest in verse four. Upright choices will cause us to flourish (vs. 11, 14). Our wealth can bring many friends, profit, and a crown (vs. 20, 23, and 24). Aren't these the things many of us and our people long for?

Often the message of stewardship and generosity are on the back of a sacrificial gift that is painful to surrender without much hope of return. Just the assurance of pure obedience alone is seen as the reward. The discipline of generosity is the preferred path of peace, provision, fulfillment, and abundance. Giving should be both a prioritized plan and a spontaneous response that is celebrated by the giver. Generosity unlocks our future instead of being bound by our own limitations or fears.

Here is great news, most people are chasing the desired blessings of God by pursuing the fruits of hard work and generosity, only we need to recognize they are found through discipleship. Not only does God desire these gifts for us, but He has a plan to provide them. He wants you to experience all He has for you and your church. God is more than willing to unleash His plan for you, in you, and through you to expand His gospel to the uttermost around the world. Nothing is too big to overcome God's gracious power to give.

What is your financial dream for yourself? What dream would you have for the people you lead and your church? I want to remind you that the power of generosity is not just an opportunity for the wealthy and privileged or the fastest growing largest churches. It is for all who are obedient.

<u>Take Away:</u> Write down what your generosity dream looks like for yourself and the people in your ministry. Review the *Staff Team Up* and come prepared to add value to your team.

STAFF TEAM UP

Set aside two to three hours and come prepared to collaborate as a team. You will need a flip chart and markers for these exercises.

Each staff member is to take a turn and share three lessons learned this week.

- What did you learn and apply from the devotions in Proverbs this week?

- What insights did you gain that can be applied to your ministry or church?

- What verse did you find on your own in Proverbs or elsewhere in Scripture that has a stewardship principle or implication?

Do you know how many non-givers, tippers, obedient, and extravagant givers are in your ministry? A staff member should bring a detailed giving report (without names of people) for all to see. Consider gathering information based on size of gift, how often people give, age of donor, service a donor attends, and how involved givers are in the life of the church. Have a time of open discussion and create a list of truthful insights that need to be addressed.

I have described four different types of givers: non-givers, tippers, obedient givers, and extravagant givers. Do you think there are more or less than four categories of givers? If so, what names would you use to describe the different categories in your ministry?

- Create a list of committed categories of givers for your church that will help you design a growth plan in the future for each one. Make them affirming and compelling.

- Provide a clear, brief description of each type of giver in a way that is identifiable and can be repeatedly measured in the future.

- Locate a couple of verses of Scripture that help describe this type of giver. Try to find verses that affirm and do not destroy.

- Create a list of potential areas of personal generosity growth for each category. These should provide you with a discipleship direction as a leader.

Illustration: *"Beginner: I give on occasion as I have resources and feel compelled."*

"In the midst of a very severe trial, their overflowing joy and their extreme poverty welled up in rich generosity." (2 Corinthians 8:2 NIV)

"Command them to do good, to be rich in good deeds, and to be generous and willing to share." (1 Timothy 6:18 NIV)

I long to grow by:

- *Understanding more about how the church uses the resources I might donate.*

- *Getting out of my current financial challenges and living a more financially free life.*

- *Moving past my prior bad experiences with the church.*

- *Learning to give more regularly.*

- *Getting closer to God, so I can trust Him more.*

WHY THIS EXERCISE IS IMPORTANT:

Learning to use language to describe the type of disciple you are leading is an extremely valuable exercise. It takes time to look behind the specific pattern of generosity to gain an adequate understanding of the need. A first grade teacher has a different approach and content than a sixth grade teacher. Once you understand to whom you are ministering and why they behave the way they do, the quicker you can develop an appropriate discipleship strategy. Delivering good content to the wrong audience goes nowhere.

For many, this is a new way of thinking. You will have to push yourself, specifically in your different areas of ministry. Do not quit or short-circuit the process. See the potential. Make sure you are growing so you can lead. Then you will be able to lead, train, teach, and organize others toward generosity growth.

WEEK 3:
YOU MAP WHERE
YOU ARE HEADED

WEEK 3

YOU MAP WHERE YOU ARE HEADED

SMALL CHURCH, USA

You may be surprised to know that small churches can be resource giants. They can be characterized by long-standing generous members, more streamlined ministry expenses, and higher levels of volunteer leadership. As a matter of fact, larger churches that live the generous life actually have to learn to embrace principles that are naturally engrained in smaller church culture. Unfortunately, many small churches are bound by limitations, both real and perceived, instead of being free to release their resources.

Simplicity, clarity, and focus are critical elements to the success of any church, but especially the small church. Being comfortable in your own skin and not worrying about trying to pull off the big church programming is a must. The two biggest line items that dominate church budgets are allocated to staff and facility expenses. A small church, which engages volunteers to do the work of paid staff, mixed with a low or non-existent mortgage payment can be freeing. Then, when a small church learns to leverage what it does best through personal care and attention, the eternal impact can leap forward dramatically.

A well-led small church should be able to give personal attention to both its members and those in need in the community. It should also be able to leverage a high degree of trust which can open many ministry doors locally. A small church can go places larger churches struggle to go, because it goes on the relationships of its members.

Just imagine the kind of impact a small church could have if it focused its resources purely on one major initiative. How much good could be done if discipling kids was a major focus? This could lead to a personal relationship with the local school, foster care, youth athletic events, the families living in poverty right down the road, and adoption of an orphanage overseas. A focused passion creates a defined discipleship strategy. The dedicated resources would release the people to accomplish more together. A powerful focus expands impact, it doesn't limit it.

Unfortunately, most small churches do not leverage their strength, but struggle with internal conflict, strive to become something they're not, or just cruise in idle week to week. Do not let smallness become an excuse for low impact. Jesus took 12 newbies and proceeded to change the world. I know you are not Jesus, but He still is.

PROVERBS 15 - IT IS GOOD TO BE CONTENT

*"Better a **little** with the fear of the Lord than **great wealth** with turmoil. Better a **small serving** of vegetables with love than a **fattened calf** with hatred." (Proverbs 15:16, 17 NIV)*

Contentment is a lifelong pursuit. It truly is hard to be content. As a matter of fact, you have to learn how to be content. Here are two words that can help: process and perspective. Contentment is not an event or experience, it is a trained discipline of the soul. Perspective is the active ingredient that enables contentment in many different trying situations.

Proverbs provides us with both. For instance, verse 19 reads, *"The way of the sluggard is blocked with thorns, but the path of the upright is a highway."* The perspective of the sluggard is different than that of the upright. The process is also contrasting in terms—that of a highway as compared with a path blocked with thorns. In verse 25, God promises to protect and provide for the widow, while in verse 27 He intends ruin for those with a greedy perspective.

Envy is one element that produces discontent. Do not look at the ministries of others and judge them wrongly just by looking at the surface. Do not measure your success based on the perceived success of others. This will deceive you, eat at you, and cause you to either quit or strive to not be yourself. You must first be content. God has a generous plan for your ministry. It will be completely different and unique. However, you must map your own journey.

I have served many churches that have existed in portable or lease situations. Many times pastors are almost embarrassed or feel like they are leading something less than a church. However, they have these amazing personal stories to tell—like the person who was far from God but is now leading the greeters, or the local school principal that calls regularly looking for support for a hurting teacher. We need to learn to be comfortable in our own skin and know that the kingdom is served by many expressions of the local church. Contentment is a great gift to yourself.

<u>Take Away:</u> Confess areas of envy and discontent. You may even need to confess that you have been staring at the way blocked with thorns and given up or blamed others. Ask God to give you courage and wisdom to see and lead a path forward.

PROVERBS 16 - LEADERSHIP AND DISCIPLESHIP

*"Honest **scales and balances** belong to the Lord; all the **weights in the bag** are of his making." (Proverbs 16:11 NIV)*

When you read this proverb, verse 11 may have been passed by as one without a stewardship implication. Scales, balances, and weights were the foundation of marketplace transactions. Their stated values created honest commerce. You had to trust that the vender was not cheating you, and as a vender you had to be trustworthy. Of course, many weren't, and that is why this verse exists.

God has established the path of commerce and the role of generosity in life. We try to solve financial problems in ways that appear to work initially, but the long-term gain is trouble. This is why we must provide solid paths of discipleship for all people to grow and guide them. Take a look at the encouragement you are provided as a leader.

*"Better a **little** with righteousness than **much** gain with injustice." (Proverbs 16:8 NIV)*

*"How much better to get **wisdom than gold**, to get **insight rather than silver!**" (Proverbs 16:16 NIV)*

*"Whoever gives **heed to instruction prospers**, and blessed is the one who trusts in the Lord." (Proverbs 16:20 NIV)*

Most churches—whether big or small—tend to lean one way or the other with their resources. They either try to do too much or too little with their resources. A church can be bound by trying to become all things to all people, thus diluting their resources. Or they can have thousands of dollars in designated funds just sitting in a bank account, thus hoarding their resources. God gives you resources to do something specific. Having wisdom to know what your church does better than 10,000 others is critical. This focus empowers and releases.

I often interact with churches that struggle to spend money, especially large sums of money. God gives you money to spend. As a matter of fact, money has one clear function, which is to be spent. It is not more obedient to allow the church facility to exist in a dated and ineffective state, because you are being frugal. This way of thinking is often bound by fear and a lack of trust, which are both sinful results of perceiving God to be small.

If you as a leader are not firmly holding an accurate scale that rightly measures and uses resources, then you are lacking stewardship wisdom. A lack of clarity and conviction will cause resources to be wrongly directed. Your people will not be discipled toward fulfillment of the vision, and they will struggle to discern their role in the kingdom at your church.

<u>Take Away:</u> Read Proverbs 16 again. Take note of every verse that speaks of your plans, God's way, and wisdom for your life path.

PROVERBS 17 - FAMILIES NEED HELP

*"Better a dry crust with peace and quiet than a house **full of feasting**, with strife." (Proverbs 17:1 NIV)*

I am sure you are aware of how money affects families. It is the cause of many arguments, pains, and disagreements. It is has been a root issue for many divorces. Money can be used as both a way to control and condemn. Children learn about money in the home more than anywhere else, so we naturally perpetuate problems or pass on healthy practices. Most families do not train their children well. If the church is a silent voice, I wonder how things will develop in the future.

I am grateful for my parents. They took me to the bank when I was a grade school boy and helped me open a savings account. Then they would take me regularly to the bank to make a deposit into the account from my chore money. The amount wasn't much, but the discipline has never left my life.

Money management is not rocket science. Spend less than you earn. Utilize a minimal amount of debt for a home or car. Strive to give 10%, save 10%, and live off the rest. Once you reach this level, you can grow beyond it. For years my family put cash in envelopes, kept every receipt, and quit spending when the envelope ran out of cash. Even as a stewardship professional, I do not have secret tools or tricks. It is basic discipleship.

Every member of the family knows the power of money. Just think for a moment of what different family members experience related to money in a given week.

- The pressure to provide

- The need to feel secure

- The car surprisingly leaves you stranded

- The sales call that doesn't go as expected

- The birthday card in the mail box

- The toy aisle and all its promises, mom and all she denies

- The dwindling retirement account

- The offering envelope that affirms obedience or exposes the opposite

- The argument, the sleepless night, the fun vacation, the new ball bat, among others

Money impacts every age group. Then, each stage in life has unique challenges and opportunities. It affects all of us mentally, emotionally, spiritually, and relationally. Everyone needs to be discipled appropriately, and the church needs a well-coordinated strategy.

Take Away: Make a list of the top three financial issues, challenges, or opportunities your families or ministry participants are facing. Be specific to the ministry area you lead.

PROVERBS 18 - IT COMES DOWN TO TRUST

*"The name of the Lord is a fortified tower; the righteous run to it and are safe. The **wealth** of the **rich** is their fortified city; they imagine it a wall too high to scale." (Proverbs 18:10, 11 NIV)*

We have learned that money can influence everything from your self-esteem to personal relationships. It can easily become the directing force in your future. Money is made of paper and metal. It doesn't take long for it to show the wear and tear of daily use. And ultimately it is lost, destroyed, or taken out of circulation.

Now, why do we let something so temporary have such influence? The mental construct and emotional experience of tipping a server has always amazed me. Most people readily give 15-20% tip when a service is rendered. We used to provide tips primarily at restaurants. Now we tip everywhere, from hotels to coffee shops to in home service providers. I am not sure it has ever crossed my mind that I might not survive financially if I provide a generous tip to a server. However, how many times does it cross a believer's mind that if I tithe I might not be able to make it? How will we ever live generous lives giving beyond the 10% point? Bold, audacious, trusting faith is required of the generous leader and follower.

If your fortified city is made of paper and metal instead of the eternal and all-powerful God, what kind of faith experience should you expect? When you trust money, self becomes the guide, and you will quickly learn your limitations. When God is seen as your ultimate provider, then the pressure is off. You are requested to be an obedient steward by faith, and God promises to be your fortified city. You choose where you live.

It is not uncommon for me to witness God being bold. I have seen more than one church receive a million dollar gift from an unsuspecting individual. God is also in the habit of granting amazing pieces of property to unsuspecting congregations. Every time I witness these surprising events it is always preceded by a pastor who has experienced God deeply in prayer and has responded with bold obedience. The submission comes before the provision.

<u>Take Away:</u> How regularly do you tell personal or corporate stories of God displaying bold miraculous action on your behalf? The church needs leaders who live dangerously and tell amazingly true stories of God's work.

PROVERBS 19 - GIVING IN THE IMAGE OF JESUS

*"Whoever is kind to the **poor** lends to the Lord, and he will **reward** them for what they have done." (Proverbs 19:17 NIV)*

The repeated theme of the life of the poor is pretty strong in chapter 19. Of course verse 17 creates an unmistakable parallel to the teachings of Jesus.

*"Truly I tell you, anyone who **gives** you a cup of water in my name because you belong to the Messiah will certainly not lose their **reward**." (Mark 9:41 NIV)*

*"He will reply, 'Truly I tell you, whatever you **did not do** for one of the least of these, you did not do for me.' Then they will go away to eternal punishment, but the righteous to **eternal life**." (Matthew 25:45, 46 NIV)*

I have often promoted in my consulting with pastors that the deepest point of discipleship is generosity. I just can't get away from the eternally generous nature of God. If we are created in His image, then born again in Christ's image, generosity must be a core pursuit.

Here are some ways God is generous:

* His willingness to create free humans

* His desire to have a deep relationship with them

- His redemption plan for creation both globally and specifically

- His time to listen to prayer

- His patience to act, respond, and continually recreate

- His grace

- His love

- His kindness

- His forgiveness

- The cross

- Heaven

The list of God's generous acts is endless. He desires this both for us and in us. However, in this world we are not wired to be generous. Our sin nature is so powerful that selfishness, fear, and distrust overwhelm the generosity of the Jesus life. The only way I know to combat this is to start being generous. Do not wait until you feel secure, rich, or even content. Start living generously today as if it was your last week on earth.

These verses in Proverbs contain both a promise and a punishment. I'm not advocating to give to get, or to give out of fear. But I would say that giving is a powerful force toward your preferred life. We tend to think our preferred life occurs when we get a sizable raise or pay off our debts. This is not true. God calls us today to our preferred lives. We have opportunities daily to be generous. When it occurs remember it is not primarily about the other person. God can care for them with or without you. Giving is about what God wants to do in you and for you.

Take Away: Note how many different references Proverbs 19 contains to the extremes of poverty and wealth. Create one central statement bringing these two extremes together.

PROVERBS 20 - IT TAKES TIME

*"Do not love sleep or you will **grow poor;** stay awake and you will have food to spare." (Proverbs 20:13 NIV)*

Americans love the quick and easy steps to success. Our media both inside and outside the church proliferate these types of stories as if they are achievable by all. While these stories can be inspiring, they also typically only tell half the truth. No one wants to hear about the long, hard journey with multiple setbacks and struggles with quitting. Because there are no stores selling seeds to grow real money trees, we have to solve the generosity issue another way.

You must choose the path of consistent discipline over time which reaps powerful results. Here are some steps you must cover:

- Discover your unique calling and vision.

- You can have confidence, because God promises to provide for His calling.

- Align your resources to the vision. This will involve saying "no" to things you and others may like a lot.

- Embrace delayed gratification. If you stick with it and do not quit, you will get there. It just may take three years instead of 30 days.

- Cast vision and disciple toward the vision.

- Grow leaders and align your ministries.

- Pray, fast, and lead boldly generous lives.

When you have clarity, alignment, and discipline you will see results. Establish some small milestones along the way to mark success. Celebrate these wins. This will keep you inspired and affirm your direction.

*"**Sluggards** do not plow in season; so at **harvest** time they look but find nothing." (Proverbs 20:4 NIV)*

*"An **inheritance** claimed too soon will not be **blessed** at the end." (Proverbs 20:21 NIV)*

Leader, here is some good news. I have had the privilege of serving on staff and as a consultant in some large churches—churches with pastors who are nationally-known and have experienced exponential growth. I want you to know it is the same everywhere I go. These leaders are normal people who are figuring it out as they go along. They have no secrets to success or growth. As a matter of fact, when God does something exponential it is not about us. We just happen to be in the right place at the right time. Once you see the back story, what is on the surface looks far less glamorous.

<u>Take Away:</u> Is your vision clearly aligning your resources (people, ministries, time, space, and money) to accomplish its goal?

PROVERBS 21 - GOD PROMISES PROFIT

"In the Lord's hand the king's heart is a stream of water that he **channels** *toward all who please him." (Proverbs 21:1 NIV)*

"The plans of the diligent lead to **profit** *as surely as haste leads to* **poverty***." (Proverbs 21:5 NIV)*

"The craving of a **sluggard** *will be the death of him, because his hands refuse to* **work***. All day long he craves for more, but the* **righteous give without sparing***." (Proverbs 21:25, 26 NIV)*

Leaders must own responsibility. It is through the leader that God directs, inspires, grows, comforts, and rewards His people. The king's heart is a stream of water. The heart of a leader is often weighed down, empty, hurting, or burned out. It can be tough for a leader to even pray or spend time with God without a church agenda, because the weight of leadership is so heavy.

The plans of the leader should lead to abundance. How does your staff and lay leadership feel when you walk into the room? Your leadership should be refreshing to those you lead and abundance should be the result.

Take a moment to reflect. Where are you personally in being a generous human being, follower of Christ, and leader of people? Is good stuff flowing through you to others naturally? If not, this is the starting point for your generous life.

Now that you have reflected, take the time to dream. What does a generous life look like for you as an individual? Please eliminate the highly unlikely scenarios of finding a million dollars or becoming a speaker to all the mega-churches. Given your unique past, experiences, location, and place in life, what does your generous life look like? Then do the same for your ministry or church.

The King has all the resources at His disposal, and His heart is turned toward you. He has a vision for your life and ministry that is way beyond your ability to think, imagine, comprehend, and definitely accomplish without Him. However, when we abide, submit, and follow the impossible becomes possible.

Move beyond the past and start embracing your future. God desires extravagant generosity for you and from you. He also wants to unleash this in your church. I promise. It is God's plan. Begin to pray daily a bold prayer of faith and chase after it with all your heart.

Take Away: Journal about your generosity vision for your life and ministry. Review the *Staff Team Up* and come prepared to add value to your team.

STAFF TEAM UP

Set aside two to three hours and come prepared to collaborate as a team. You will need a flip chart and markers for these exercises.

Each staff member take a turn and share three lessons learned this week.

- What did you learn and apply from the devotions in Proverbs this week?

- What insights did you gain that can be applied to your ministry or church?

- What verse did you find on your own in Proverbs or elsewhere in Scripture that has a stewardship principle or implication?

At this time you should have created some values to shape your culture and some measures as an end goal. Now, it is time to create your discipleship strategy. Select one area of ministry like "worship" and make an exhaustive list of the different ministry ideas that can help set the tone for a generous culture.

- Think in terms of your normal rhythm of weekly, monthly, periodic, and annual opportunities to naturally inject a generosity language.

- Repeat this exercise for other ministries such as small groups, communication, administration, and missions.

- During these exercises remember you have previously worked on both values and measures of generosity. They should flavor and direct your planning.

Illustration: *"Worship"*

- *Weekly we can pray for the financial needs of our people. We can read a generosity Scripture. We can share background facts to boost confidence about how our church handles money.*

- *Monthly we can have a testimony or highlight a ministry tying in the generosity component.*

- *Periodically we can have special offerings that highlight unique areas of our vision and needs in our city.*

- *Annually* we can host an inspiring time celebrating the work of God through us demonstrating alignment of time, energy, and resources for dramatic impact.

WHY THIS EXERCISE IS IMPORTANT:

I want you to remember back toward our opening assignment. You were to create an initial discipleship path that led a first-time guest to grow into a generous disciple. That exercise was intended in part to reveal that a generous culture was the responsibility of every ministry. It is not just for the accounting office to force us to spend less and the pastor to preach more about money.

I hope that you created at least one value that resonates with each staff member and ministry area. You should also know the different types of givers in your church, where they are involved, and what discipleship needs they have. The last step is to create a practical strategy in each area of ministry that can be accomplished over the course of three years to grow a generous disciple that can be uniquely engaged in your church to fulfill your specific vision. All ministries working in alignment will experience amazing results.

Just as there are no secrets to financial success, the same is true of ministry. You must plan the work and work the plan. Growing disciples grow leaders who develop ministries that transform society.

WEEK 4:
YOU CAN BECOME
WHAT YOU ENVISION

WEEK 4

YOU CAN BECOME WHAT YOU ENVISION

THE GENEROUS CHURCH, USA

Generous churches come in all sizes, styles, and shapes. They all go about it uniquely, but the end result is the same. Here is the key: it starts at the top. The senior leader is disciplined with his own money and that of his church. He has chosen the lifestyle of an obedient steward long before the financial crisis arises. He has earned, given, and saved. The church he leads looks the same. I know the church is in good hands when the pastor knows his numbers inside and out. He knows the patterns of spending as well as the levels of generosity. He knows when and where to invest for the greatest return. Disobedience with resources and poor stewardship move him to repentance first, not anger.

The budget planning process is different. Instead of each staff member submitting a request for their ministry above last year's amount, a team of trained leaders set the priorities. The activity of God over the past year, specific visionary milestones moving forward, and current needs drive the conversation. The spending plan is set boldly, yet conservatively, in alignment with the vision instead of the standard "faith" increase to support the ever-expanding dream.

The generosity plan takes several elements into account, from the older AC unit which may need to be replaced to the surprise benevolent need. It is known that God will bless along the way and call to expand the ministry. There will also be a crisis. It happens every year, and the church will be prepared to pray faithfully through it.

A new venture will be announced. There will be a partnership with a foreign mission organization to work with other congregations to construct an orphanage. The role will be small at first, but feel so big because of the scope of the organization we are supporting. This will be the first step into a larger mission expression down the road.

Every weekend just prior to the offering time, the church will celebrate the generosity and obedience of our people. They will give and invest wisely. The conversation will be bold, positive, and full of appreciation. Along the way, the leaders will ask the church to pray about giving above and beyond their regular offerings to a special cause. The leaders train them to have a sensitive heart to the Holy Spirit. The leaders will support it with a season of prayer followed by generosity. Then the church will celebrate the fruit.

Along the way, leaders will remind people of what great care is taken in how money is spent. The leaders will remind them how much is saved, invested in ministry, and given away. The leaders will help them gain confidence and be proud. Then when the generosity flows, they will not alter the spending plan, but save the resources.

The generous church makes sure to invest in future leaders. They are willing to go the furthest the fastest, so they will get insider information, transformational stories, and regular updates of progress. They will be empowered, affirmed, and engaged to tackle the next mountain top.

This positive and healthy culture will open people to wanting to do more. They will grow like never before and be looking for opportunities to bless. We need to have our ministries ready to train, equip, disciple, and release. We may actually have more people looking to live bigger lives than ever before.

PROVERBS 22 - CHURCH AND DEBT

*"The **rich** rule over the **poor**, and the **borrower** is slave to the **lender**." (Proverbs 22:7 NIV)*

Debt is a huge topic at the church, both theologically and practically. It can be seen as the ultimate sin or the ultimate goal. The Bible never declares debt as a sin and certainly not the unforgivable financial sin. Nor does it ever set up that obedient stewardship begins once a person is debt free. Debt certainly can be a sign of lack of trust or hard work. It can be the result of rewarding a wrong impulse. Managed debt can also be a responsible choice. Obedient stewardship both personally and corporately does not begin and end with the issue of being debt free.

Now, the single most limiting category that keeps church finances from freedom is how much a church invests in facilities. This includes such expenses as a mortgage, utilities, maintenance, insurance, and expansion. Committing to a building means that the church is embracing a wide array of fixed costs. This means that all other costs must flex, like missions, ministry, and personnel.

The church does exist outside the building and certainly can flourish without a permanent structure in many parts of the world. However, most churches in America will need to invest significant dollars in a facility. The average church, which maintains a manageable debt load, usually expends about 25% or less of its income on its facility. If the church has recently engaged in a significant building project or has over-built in the past, that number can be 30-35%. Unfortunately, there are stories that are even more extreme.

Here is the simple science for wise facility investment. First, you should always build for growth. The right facility, at the right time, done the right way, in the right location produces numeric results. Next, you should under-build. When you under-build you are keeping your debt load as low as possible. This enables more freedom in the future. Under-building forces you to run multiple services and develop a larger leadership base. This numeric and leadership growth increases cash flow. When an increased cash flow meets a strong leadership base and a low debt ratio, you are on the verge of potential. Finally, always build with the next step in mind. Every growing church will reach a point where it embraces a project that defines its future. Often the building cost embraced is so high it limits the opportunities moving ahead. One day you will not be able to build a bigger building, but you will still be called to expand the kingdom. What will you do then? And are you getting ready for that day?

Take Away: Consider what steps your church can take to move into a more flexible and powerful cash flow position.

PROVERBS 23 - DISCOVER YOUR UNIQUE GENEROSITY FUTURE

*"Do not wear yourself out to **get rich**; do not trust your own cleverness."*
(Proverbs 23:4 NIV)

Impatience and self-reliance are two big factors that impact church leaders. I see it in a few different ways. It can be the young pastor who does not have the perspective of how much time it takes for a process to produce natural results. Other times I see it in a pastor who is struggling with perceived failure, so he is always kick-starting new ideas. Then there is the insecure pastor who is trying to prove himself a successful leader as if the results of the church were on his shoulders. Patience, prayer, diligence, and knowing what God has specifically called you to do are critical. Learning not to wear yourself out is a worthwhile pursuit.

If you have not been living as a generous leader of a generous church, then it is going to take some time. First, God measures success differently, so you may need to change your measuring stick. He sees today, tomorrow, and eternity. He has it all under control. If a church of 50 is meeting in a school and baptizing disciples while making community impact, is it bringing more or less glory to God than a church of 25,000? We know the answer. Churches of all sizes can give God glory.

The model of a generous church comes in all shapes and sizes. We need to patiently pursue God's unique calling as our part of the kingdom. We need to cooperate with His people down the road and around the world to present the complete gospel to those who are not walking with Him. Your church has a generous future that is God's perfect design. It will have some similar fundamental principles of other churches, but the expression will be uniquely yours.

*"There is surely a **future hope** for you, and your hope **will not be cut off.**"* (Proverbs 23:18 NIV)

To embrace your unique future you will have to make some hard value choices. This can be difficult for you and your leadership. Generosity ministry is a mountain to climb, not a sprint to run. One of the first steps is to get spending in order. I would encourage you to set a goal that your future annual ministry budget will total 90% of your previous year's receipts. Then with this 90% establish 80% for internal expenses, 10% for giving to outside causes, and 10% for cash reserves. When churches are able to achieve this, the future begins to become reality. The alternative is to set a "faith" budget every year, raise "visionary" expenses, and live with the stressful results.

Take Away: If you chose to exist on 90% of your previous year's receipts, what would be the hardest decision you would have to make? Would it be worth it over the long run?

PROVERBS 24 - PREPARE YOUR LEADERSHIP

*"Put your **outdoor work** in order and **get your fields** ready; after that, **build your house.**"* (Proverbs 24:27 NIV)

Climbing a mountain takes one small step at a time, and it typically is not a journey straight up the steepest face. If the majority of us are going to reach a peak on foot, it is going to involve a clear, well-marked, and winding path that avoids unnecessary danger. We will want to have plenty of water along the way and need a team of people to keep us motivated.

Becoming a generous church is impossible without a complete team effort. Putting your outdoor work in order is critical. You gather workers and supplies. You equip them to accomplish the task. The fields are then prepared before the seeds are planted. The growth is cultivated after the seeds are planted. After the growth is cultivated, the crops arrive. However, it all started with preparing the team.

Speaking of your team, it is not uncommon for a church to spend on average 50% of its receipts on personnel expenses. I have seen this figure as high as 80% by a small church plant and as low as 25% by a mega-church. Just like a mortgage payment can create either an exponential growth opportunity or extreme financial constraint, the staff expense can have a significant impact.

However, the difference between a mortgage and staff is important to note. One is a fixed expense and the other is optional. Churches that live in a generous mode have a committed leadership culture. They hire strategically by skill set and impact. They also equip and empower both bi-vocational and volunteer staff. They are willing to make the hard call of de-enlisting or helping a staff member quickly find their ultimate place of service elsewhere. I know it can be difficult to release staff. There is the assumption of senior leadership failing in the wrong hire, the pain it will cause a ministry, and the family being directly affected. However, if a particular individual is not in their perfect ministry fit and you are spending God's resources on him or her, it is an unwise choice.

I can attest as someone who has lost a job that it was the best decision for me. It didn't feel fun for me or the organization at the time, but it was definitely God's design for both, and I am so grateful.

*"Know also that **wisdom** is like honey for you: If you find it, there is a **future hope** for you, and your hope will not be cut off." (Proverbs 24:14 NIV)*

<u>Take Away:</u> Note verses 5-6, 19-20, and 30-34. In what areas do you need to begin to seek the wisdom of others on your staff and leadership to help you achieve your dream future?

PROVERBS 25 - LEARN ABOUT YOUR ROI

*"Like clouds and wind **without rain** is one who boasts of **gifts never given."** (Proverbs 25:14 NIV)*

Over the last few years there have been some interesting developments in volunteerism and charitable giving. I first noticed a shift when 9/11 occurred. This was a most dramatic and catastrophic experience for Americans. It caused us to feel vulnerability as well as a swell of pride and brotherly love. We quickly moved to the rescue of our citizens who volunteered both in the city and to serve our country. In the years to follow, we would experience natural disasters like Katrina and tornadoes ripping across our land. The media would also begin to gravitate towards global issues and causes. Serving the needs of the world and our cities has become commonplace language in modern society.

You may have noticed the generosity conversation has become common vernacular. Most businesses have relationships with multiple non-profits. Serving and giving is promoted in the workplace as good for the individual, the team, and the community. The airwaves, commercials, television, and its stars are widely promoting their latest cause in dramatic fashion. Your people are being solicited at work, at school, and at home. They are hearing compelling stories, seeing powerful results, and being invited to live a life of impact. Then we have the story they hear at church.

This has obviously produced a fair amount of competition for donations. Over the past few years, charitable donations for every segment, like education, health care, and global causes are on the rise. However, giving to religious groups is on the decline. People are desiring to live bigger lives today. The ministries that tell their stories in clear and compelling ways are rising to the top.

It could be assumed that the church is supposed to be the most giving organization in the community. However, its community gift is often traffic jams, crowded restaurants, and decreasing land values of its neighbors. While the church should not brag or boast about all it does, it should know its vision, purpose, story, and results well. That story should be the cultural language and lifestyle week in and week out. Once this culture exists, the results will speak for themselves.

Possess a clear vision. Make giving easy. Focus your resources. Celebrate your victories. Be a fan of your city. Give people steady opportunities to live big lives together.

Take Away: What are your signature stories of invested time, money, energy, passion, or prayer?

PROVERBS 26 - LANGUAGE IS POWERFUL

*"Sending a **message** by the hands of a fool is like cutting off one's feet or drinking poison." (Proverbs 26:6 NIV)*

One of the most powerful tools a leader possesses is language. Yet, it is one of the most commonly overlooked assets of vision. Just think for a moment about how influential language is in your ability to function on a day-to-day basis. For example, when a newborn is brought into the home, the child knows one mode of communication, crying. But those cries can mean any number of things from "I'm tired" to "I'm hungry" to "I'm messy." Each need requires a different response. Until you meet the need accurately, the crying continues. The language challenge can continue throughout life. As a child gets older they share "My stomach hurts." Well, does that mean you're hungry or you ate too much? Or, are you sick and need to go to bed or to the Emergency Room? As a grown up if you have ever tried to order a meal from a menu not written in English, or tried to comprehend your doctor's diagnosis, or even worse your computer tech's remedy, you know firsthand how critical language is.

Language directs, teaches, inspires, unifies, and instructs. When it comes to money language at church, it typically comes in a few different dialects. When pastors are uncomfortable with the topic there is silence and even light-heartedness. When there is a need it is usually communicated in terms of the budget, building, or crisis. However, you need to develop a money language of vision and discipleship.

Simply, language is a free and powerful tool. Don't be caught sending the biblical stewardship message via a fool.

Consider some ways you can begin to discover and introduce a healthy language related to money.

- Tell a personal story about a money challenge you have faced. The process of how you worked through it should be human and identifiable by all.

- Provide an illustration from common culture about how people, companies, or organizations are living generous lives. It is so easy to find stories today of unassuming people doing simple things to make a powerful impact. Remember it is not about the size of the gift, but that it is relatable to life.

- Read a book on either personal or corporate money management. Have a discussion with business leaders in your church about how these truths impact their lives. This will provide you with another perspective you do not currently possess.

<u>Take Away:</u> Proverbs 26 contains several references to language, the mouth, and the tongue. It also contains several verses that apply directly to stewardship. Locate these verses to help broaden your perspective on leading a generous church.

PROVERBS 27 - DISCIPLING KEY GIVERS

*"Be sure you know the condition of your flocks, give careful attention to your herds; for **riches** do not endure forever, and a **crown** is not secure for all generations." (Proverbs 27:23, 24 NIV)*

Possibly the most intimidating mountain to climb in leading a generous church is to learn how to disciple key donors. Pastors can come at this from polarizing positions. Some want to know nothing regarding a person's capacity to give, while others want all the details. Whatever your position you need to understand that all people need to be discipled in the spiritual discipline of giving. I am all for serving the poor because scripture calls us to it, but I am also for strategically discipling those at the other end of the financial spectrum.

Those that earn above average salaries have significant emotional and spiritual needs that only another leader can meet. I have a good friend who is wealthy, and I remember the first time I took him to lunch. At the end he looked across the table and said, "Do you know that I can't remember the last time someone bought me lunch? People are always looking to me for something and this was nice. Thank you." He was longing for a friend and a level playing field, because he could not find that in his company or at his church.

Key donors are typically high capacity leaders and can have an intimidating exterior persona. However, they need personal discipleship by another key leader. In the local church that is the pastor. So pastors, you need to make sure you are growing as a leader, work to understand the business world, make sure you lead the business of the church well, and boldly invest in the key leaders in your church. I would even take it a step further and let them mentor you in business, finances, and staff development.

"As iron sharpens iron, so one person sharpens another." (Proverbs 27:17 NIV)

Not only can key donors be somewhat disconnected from the mainstream of the church, they can also find it difficult to volunteer. Discipling a key donor will involve creating new ministry positions. Most high capacity leaders will not be motivated by serving on the benevolence team, being a greeter, or even leading a small group. They will want to blaze a new trail or lead a massive effort. Their schedules will be busy, but it doesn't take much time for a high stakes individual to accomplish a great task. Discipleship is part relationship, part content, and part practice. You will need to find some meaningful places of service. This will release both growth and resources.

Take Away: Make a list of 10 key leaders in whom you will begin to invest.

PROVERBS 28 - BE DECISIVE AND PATIENT

*"The wicked flee though no one pursues, but the righteous are as **bold** as a lion." (Proverbs 28:1 NIV)*

*"When a country is rebellious, it has many rulers, but a ruler with discernment and knowledge maintains **order**." (Proverbs 28:2 NIV)*

*"Those who **work** their land will have **abundant** food, but those who chase fantasies will have their fill of **poverty**." (Proverbs 28:19 NIV)*

I promise that God has an abundantly generous future for your church. He has a vision for impact and the resources you need. And God is even ready to make sure you have them when you are ready to properly use them. Of course, the alternative is to live in a high stress, under resourced, and intimidating financial position.

Wise financial management is not rocket science. It is actually pretty basic. Here is a reminder of several items we have discussed:

- Discern God's unique vision for your church.

- Over time focus all of your resources, staff, buildings, finances, and ministries.

- Say "no" to whatever is not in line with your vision.

- Learn to live on 90% of last year's receipts.

- Give at least 10% away to like-minded causes.

- Save at least 10% yearly until you have three to six months' expenses in cash reserves.

- Patiently wait, stick to the plan, and get ready to start saying "yes" to new ventures.

- Grow generous disciples of all ages.

- Possess a high leadership culture.

- Pray, lead, and ask boldly.

Just imagine the staff meeting or budget-planning process in which the discussions aren't about cuts, aren't about what you can't do, and aren't about turning off the lights to save money. It can happen; churches all over the country are, in fact, continually ready for God's next assignment. They have a ready "yes" waiting for God's call. This can be you too. It may be painful at first to make some spending adjustments, but you must be bold. God blesses obedience. And if you are boldly discipling your members the conversation will change in a relatively short period of time.

Generosity is possible; it is God-designed. It starts with leaders who are willing to make bold decisions.

Take Away: Make a list of three bold decisions you need to consider making this year. Review the *Staff Team Up* and come prepared to add value to your team.

STAFF TEAM UP

Set aside two to three hours and come prepared to collaborate as a team. You will need a flip chart and markers for these exercises.

Each staff member take a turn and share three lessons learned this week.

- What did you learn and apply from the devotions in Proverbs this week?

- What insights did you gain that can be applied to your ministry or church?

- What verse did you find on your own in Proverbs or elsewhere in Scripture that has a stewardship principle or implication?

Discuss with your staff what a realistic—yet bold—financial dream would be for your church, and give yourself three years to accomplish it or make significant headway toward it. Speak in terms of both a qualitative goal that can direct discipleship and a quantitative goal that will direct planning.

- Create yearly milestones that will need to be achieved stepping yourself to your ultimate goal.

- Create a punch list of decisions to be made in the next six months.

- Spend time calendaring the work you did previously on your discipleship strategy integrating it with your newly formed milestones.

Illustration: *"3 Year Mountain Top Dream"*

Goal: To create an inspiring giving culture that results in 50% of our people living from an obedient spending plan, six months church expenses in cash reserves, and 20% of receipts annually budgeted toward mission efforts.

Year 1 Milestone

To train our staff, begin creating a positive culture, discover/create the tools necessary to enable our people to begin their stewardship journey, and reallocate the easiest church budget expenses possible.

Year 2 Milestone

Launch a church-wide generosity discipleship emphasis, align budget to increase cash reserves to three months, and designate 15% of our resources to missions.

Year 3 Milestone

Launch a third service with age-graded small groups and volunteer opportunities, expand our leadership gifts depth, increase savings to six months, and designate 20% or our resources for missions.

WHY THIS EXERCISE IS IMPORTANT:

Focus expands; it does not limit. When your entire staff agrees to the mission, team cooperation increases dramatically. When the entire team is focused on the same goal, exponential results become possible. It is easy for individuals to exist in silos. These silos create both ignorance of the realities, unhealthy competition for resources, and diminishing returns.

Everyone is responsible for fulfilling the mission together. When sacrifice is called for, it is so much easier to embrace when you know what the win is. Otherwise it just feels like a lack of support. Every church will fill their calendars with activities that consume time and resources. Most often churches exist with good, but disconnected activities. These full calendars result in unfocused resources and unclear measures of success.

It will take a concerted effort to learn new patterns of behavior and hold yourself accountable to the long-term plan. Without committed goals and time frames, you can find yourself talking a good game but not reaping the results.

CLOSING THOUGHTS: OVERFLOW

CLOSING THOUGHTS

OVERFLOW

PROVERBS 29 - VISION CLARITY

*"Where there is no revelation, people cast off restraint; but **blessed** is the one who heeds wisdom's instruction." (Proverbs 29:18 NIV)*

Vision work is generosity work. Vision is not a cliché or catchy slogan. It's not a memorized mantra or a pipe dream. Vision is the passionate all-out pursuit of God's unique calling. If vision cannot be powerfully spoken, clearly understood, practically strategized, tangibly measured, and collectively inspired, then it is not vision.

My experience is that most leaders are too over-confident in their ability to clearly discern, articulate, and enact vision. Even when vision comes naturally, it still can be a challenging resource to manage. At

Auxano, we use five simple questions *(The Five Irreducible Questions of Leadership)* to help leaders think through the different components of an inspiringly strategic vision.

Here are the questions:

- What are we doing? State it in a stunningly unique way in 10 words or less. It is a reframing of the Great Commission based on your unique place, people, and passions.

- Why are we doing it? This speaks to the unique values of your leadership and organization. These flavor why you do things the way you do them. For instance, some churches naturally prioritize programming excellence while others may be driven more by authenticity.

- How are we doing it? This is your strategy to grow disciples that naturally accomplish the vision together. These steps direct your resources.

- When are we successful? Most churches completely miss this one. You need to articulate the measurable disciplines in the life of a Christ follower that are necessary to fulfill the mission. This should drive your teaching and ministry planning.

- Where are we headed? This question helps us clearly see our horizon in both the immediate and distant future.

It is easy to be a copy-cat vision-caster. However, God made no two people alike, and I would say the same for churches. People give to passion, hurt, and success. Learning to speak this language and lead in this way is the baseline for generosity.

<u>Take Away:</u> Give some thought to the five questions above. Does your organization possess powerfully clear answers?

PROVERBS 30 - SMALL TURNS TO BIG

*"Keep falsehood and lies far from me; give me neither **poverty nor riches**, but give me only my **daily bread**. Otherwise, I may have too much and disown you and say, 'Who is the Lord?' Or I may become **poor** and steal, and so dishonor the name of my God." (Proverbs 30:8-9 NIV)*

I have been a part of many visionary projects that required enormous faith and have learned that they never work out like you think, but they do work out. Many obstacles stand in the way of progress. At times they can seem insurmountable, like the price to relocate or the key lay person that is leading a subversive movement. Obstacles can be uncontrollable, like city policies or as painful as a staff moral failure. Not to mention the spiritual intensity of Satan and his deception that works to derail good efforts of churches. The powers of darkness can get creative in their sabotage.

All of the above and many more facets of strategic leadership create a series of difficult decisions. Success is not usually found in a surprise, miraculous moment. Most often it is one faith-based prayerful decision after another that wins over the long haul. Small things done right create unstoppable momentum.

*"Four things on earth are **small**, yet they are extremely wise: Ants are creatures of **little** strength, yet they **store** up their food in the summer" (Proverbs 30:24, 25 NIV).*

Please don't show up to your next leadership meeting and announce a hasty, dramatic change. Nor should you look at your situation and consider it a lost cause. Nothing is too big or small. God has a kingdom plan that must be fulfilled. He has put you in this time and place to experience His success.

It is easy to allow our eyes to be fixed on what isn't, what could be, or even what may never be. We must focus on our daily bread. What do I need to do today to be obedient? Tomorrow will have both its worries and provisions all to its own.

Take Away: What are the pending decisions or discussions your church will be engaging over the next six months? What natural opportunities do they provide to grow a more generous culture?

PROVERBS 31 - WHAT'S YOUR CITY SAYING ABOUT YOUR CHURCH?

*"Honor **her** for all that **her** hands have done, and let **her** works bring **her** praise at the city gate." (Proverbs 31:31 NIV)*

This is possibly the most well-known of all Proverbs, the epilogue of a noble woman or wife. Well, you are leading the bride of Christ, so we have some applications to make. Here are just a few parallels. It may be a helpful exercise for you to create a more complete list.

- The bride of Christ is more valuable than precious gems. (v. 10)

- The bride of Christ brings good not harm. (v. 12)

- The bride of Christ works with eager hands. (v. 13)

- The bride of Christ saves and invests resources in high-risk ventures. (v. 16)

- The bride of Christ is prepared for the next big task. (v. 17)

- The bride of Christ sees inspiring results from its work. (v. 18)

I think you are getting the point. However, the last verse in Proverbs is potentially the most powerful. It is a telling and an unbelievable summary to the entire book. What if God intended all of Proverbs to point to this one diagnostic question derived from the final verse?

"What is your city saying about your life and your church?"

You lead both, right?

<u>Take Away:</u> What has God done personally in your life as you have ventured through this journey in Proverbs? Are you ready to take the first step in becoming a more generous person, leader, and church?

STAFF TEAM UP

Set aside two to three hours and come prepared to collaborate as a team. You will need a flip chart and markers for these exercises.

Each staff member take a turn and share three lessons learned this week.

- What did you learn and apply from the devotions in Proverbs this week?

- What insights did you gain that can be applied to your ministry or church?

- What verse did you find on your own in Proverbs or elsewhere in Scripture that has a stewardship principle or implication?

Divide into groups and take a stab at answering the *Five Irreducible Questions of Leadership*. What similarities or differences did you uncover? Do you possess vision clarity based on the results of this exercise?

THE FIVE IRREDUCIBLE QUESTIONS OF LEADERSHIP:

- What are we doing?

- Why are we doing it?

- How are we doing it?

- When are we successful?

- Where are we headed?

Have each staff member pretend they are a local journalist who is writing a post about your church. The point of the article is to describe your church's impact on the city. Use Proverbs 31 as a guide for practical attributes of the bride of Christ the journalist could expect to see. Share these articles.

Decide as a staff what the most important bold decision is that you must make in the next 90 days to begin your journey of creating a more generous culture.

APPENDICES

APPENDIX 1

LAUNCHING A CHURCH-WIDE JOURNEY

A discipleship journey is not a short-run campaign. Campaigns certainly have their importance and should be a part of a comprehensive generosity strategy. However, I want to give you some ideas about how you can launch a yearlong initiative to grow generous disciples, including a potential message series and commitment time.

Here is how a yearlong calendar may look. You will know your seasons of financial planning and spending far better than I. The timeline would be impacted if your fiscal year is not the calendar year or if you are congregational led requiring budget approval.

JANUARY

- Begin the year offering a few financial money management classes. The holidays will have recently ended. People may have overspent or made a New Year's resolution related to finances. You may also benefit from some of the vision items you discussed in the previous fall.

- Your finance office will be sending contribution statements to every donor. This is a great vision casting opportunity. You may prepare a letter to accompany the statement along with an Annual Ministry Report. Be appreciative, share stories of success, and cast vision for continued giving.

FEBRUARY

- Create a calendar to celebrate generosity in worship. This can include an expression during a prayer time, scripture reading, personal testimony, or celebration of a ministry.

MARCH

- Conduct a church-wide serve day across your city or community.

- Launch a ministry to begin discipling high capacity leaders and those with the gift of giving.

APRIL

- Many churches are giving away their entire offering at Easter to local, national, and foreign non-profits. You will probably have several events over the summer like youth camp, kids camp, or mission trips that may need scholarship funding.

MAY

- Host a church-wide leadership event that is worshipful, prayerful, and celebrative. Appreciate and reward your volunteers for the impact they made during the recent ministry season.

JUNE

- Summer is a great time to focus on behind-the-scenes administrative planning. Give attention to your systems for counting, posting, reporting, and budgeting. Discover what metrics you can consistently measure that will help you have defined targets for successfully developing generous disciples.

JULY

- Begin to dream about the objectives, initiatives, or points of focus for your next fiscal year. Annual budget planning can begin shortly.

- Make a list of new streamlined procedures for budgeting along with a list of expenses that need to be prioritized for either an increase or decrease.

- Conduct a spiritual gifts, talents, passions, and experiences Discovery Class to help people discern where God has called them to live generously. Ministries need to be prepared to engage people in passionate areas of service.

AUGUST

- A focused attention can be brought to generosity toward children and youth as school returns and local athletic leagues begin to take shape. Adopt a school or local league to bless with generosity.

SEPTEMBER

- Budget planning should be in full force.

OCTOBER

- Launch a message series and season of prayer on a topic that will cultivate a more generous heart. Do not make money the theme, but something supportive like living with gratitude or listening to God.

NOVEMBER

- Host a church-wide celebration event that is worshipful, prayerful, and inspiring. Appreciate and reward your congregation for the impact they made during the year. This is a great time to cast vision and recruit volunteers for next year's opportunities.

- Print a full color Annual Ministry Report, create an inspiring video, and future commitment card to support the work of this month.

- Budget planning and a strategic ministry plan for the future year should be concluded.

- Launch a vision and generosity message series.

- Be prepared for the holiday season will be filled with benevolent opportunities.

DECEMBER

- Conduct a year-end offering toward a dedicated cause.

APPENDIX 2

THOUGHTS ON A GENEROSITY SERMON SERIES

At some point in time in your generosity journey you will most likely launch a church-wide emphasis. Most churches will incorporate a yearly message series as a part of their overall strategy. Of course, this will not be the only message or messages related to stewardship, but I thought I would stir some thoughts in the preachers.

Here are some practical applications, tools, and opportunities you can employ along the way:

- Reveal the different types of givers you have identified in your church and Scripture.

- Launch a few discipleship classes to support growth in the different types of givers.

- Inform your church on the many different ways they can give.

- Plan and allow for immediate participation in a special offering or tithe challenge.

- Share about the integrity standards and practices your church lives by related to money.

- Share the story of how God has worked in the past at your church related to generosity (include all mediums like live story, video, print, and digital means).

- Cast vision for the next year (you may reveal your future budget as a part of this process).

- Conclude the multi-week series with a commitment time to participate in an offering and grow as a generous disciple over the next 12 months.

Message #1: *Exodus 32:1-10 "The Golden Calves"*

This is undoubtedly my favorite stewardship passage. It begins with God's people on the other side of an amazing series of miracles. I don't need to go through the history here, you know how they were slaves and miraculously delivered. Now they are on the first day of the rest of their lives. They have come down from the euphoric high and have begun to look at one another.

They're wondering, where did our leader go? What are we going to do to sustain ourselves? Where will we live? Where are we going? Who will defend us? These are all natural and basic questions that we all experience. Their response is rather interesting.

They created their own campaign to pool their resources together to solve a soul problem. They replaced their God with created idols. Keep in mind they only had what they took with them, they struggled for food, water, and future security. Never mind all that! All they wanted was a sense of peace and security in their soul. They willingly sacrificed their resources for what was a hopefully long-term, satisfying, spiritual experience. It wasn't.

Here are some points you may consider when crafting your talk:

- We all struggle feeling secure in life. We regularly experience fear, insecurity, and a lack of purpose.

- We are all willing to make whatever sacrifices necessary to gain peace for the moment. The emotions of the moment typically rule over the long haul. We usually react to the pain instead of being patiently led by truth. We live according to our level of discipleship.

- We can look to people for help who appear to have it more together than we do and be misdirected. There was a great difference between Moses and Aaron in this story. We lead at work, at home, and in our community.

- We can make choices with our resources based on our feelings that affect our soul. Money has spiritual influence and should be spiritually influenced.

- We can miss out on God's great plan for our lives when we listen to the wrong messages. God had a divine plan that He was giving to Moses. The people are at least temporarily missing out.

I wouldn't use these phrases as points, but I would want to reveal that our emotions, people, culture, and resources can mislead us. Your people already know the pain of money. They work so hard, feel as if they have so little, and the needs ahead are daunting. They have fought about it, been fired over it, felt pressure to perform, and watched their kids get hurt by it. It won't take much to allow this passage to expose some common longings in life.

I would not want to leave the message with a great downer. As a matter of fact, I would probably only make the preceding content half of the sermon. For the second half of the sermon, I would share about God's preferred future for our souls and resources. Most people get that God wants to redeem their souls and that He wants them to tithe. However, they have little clue of what an abundantly free and blessed generous life is like.

Provide them with the inspiration of God's ability to care for them and multiply their joy through becoming a faithful steward.

- God owns everything. He had previously heard their cry and gained their release from Pharaoh. Pharaoh did not own their lives and future. God did.

- God has planned for everything, from your greatest sins to your smallest daily expenses. You can obviously point to Jesus and the cross at this point. The Lord's Prayer is an especially powerful example of God caring for every element of our lives, including our grand purpose within His kingdom.

- God has a plan to produce lasting peace and abundant fruit through each of us. I would remind them of what God's intentions were at the moment. God was seeking to establish a significant covenant relationship with His people. The Law was coming, and the Promised Land was ahead.

I would end the message with an invitation to go on the journey together. Are you ready to go on a journey that could change your life, family, and church forever? We will be discovering how God has a plan for the longings of our souls to live purposeful and fulfilled lives. All of us have gotten a little or a lot distracted, maybe even constructed a few idols of our own.

Message #2: *Exodus 31:1-11 "The Building of the Tabernacle"*

I love the context of the story in Exodus 32. God actually knew in advance that His people would be struggling with some soul issues. So before the pain hit and sin resulted (see Exodus 32 message), He provided direction and support. While Moses was on top of the mountain getting instruction from God, the people should have been joining their resources together to create a meaningful place for God's people to connect with Him. He actually provides the detail plan beginning in Exodus 25. He also creates the leadership structure, timing, and resources to accomplish His plan for their lives. God knew His people were short on discipleship and high on stress. He knew they needed an anchor for their community and a purpose for their lives. He also knew they just needed to do something productive. He was trying to help everyone out. Having said that, we all know what ended up occurring.

Here are some points you may consider when crafting your sermon:

- God knows your story today, but is not limited by it.

- God is actively preparing both you and your future.

- God has called you to be a part of something much bigger than you can imagine.

- God wants your eyes to see clearly, your heart to live boldly, and your hands to be ready.

In your sermon, bring to light the different people in the story. There was Moses who was the foster child, stuttering, murderer turned experienced leader. He had a mature faith and a special relationship with God, though that was not always the case. Bezalel and Oholiab were the ordinary leaders. They were men with a growing faith that had committed to utilizing their day-to-day experiences and resources toward a bigger life. Then there are the Israelites. The former slaves who are just beginning their lives of freedom, exploring God's plan. Everyone had a place, purpose, and opportunity to live a big life.

I would then take the opportunity to share with your church the different kinds of givers you have identified in scripture and in your church from your walk through Proverbs. (See Staff Team Up in week two) Share about the characteristics of the different types of givers, their past experiences, and patterns. Help people find their place in the journey. They should be able to positively identify themselves and have hope about their future.

You may want to move them toward a powerful example of the diversity of people in the kingdom. The kingdom consists of all walks of life that when brought together can do something amazing, like provide an opportunity for another person to connect with God. This was God's goal in Exodus 31.

I think it is important that people know what they can do next. Generosity steps tend to be the same regardless of the size of the gift. The journey goes something like this:

- Surrender your resources to the One who owns them and realize your place as a steward.

- Gain a sensitive heart to the Spirit, His leadings, and the opportunities to respond around you.

- Ask God to increase your faith and obedience, because fear will always be present.

You may consider highlighting some programming items like:

- A printed handout that is professionally created and full color. Name, define, and provide scriptural support for the different types of givers.

- Provide a few easy growth steps that people can take quickly or in the near future.

- Do not shame, guilt, or overwhelm. Help them celebrate and have hope, but also be invited to move forward.

- Issue a call to prayer.

Message #3: *Exodus 32:11-35 "Pain and Repentance"*

There is so much that happens between Exodus 32 and 34. I am not sure how long a typical sermon series lasts at your church, or how deeply you want to go into some challenging topics. I would place the overall theme of this story as learning to own your financial failings or the consequences of financial sins. Moses employs some traditional means like repentance through prayer and some not so friendly ways like decapitation.

I would tackle it one of the following ways. You may need to discern how much help you need to provide your people given the financial challenges they uniquely face.

- Redeem the topic of money. For many, finance is a painful and negative subject. Some may even view money as bad. Most will not have a healthy view of God and money. I would unpack how money is a gift from God to provide for us, bless us, and bless others. Money is to add to our lives and not take away. It is only what we do with money that can be harmful.

- Redeem from some common financial mistakes or pains. What would be the financial challenges that most commonly bind your city and congregation? Young couples may be chasing an unreasonable dream or struggling with no financial training. A man may have achieved high levels in his career, but wrecked his home. An older couple may be doing without, because they have no family to help. Speak to the specific pains and failures that uniquely bind your people and city. Obviously, you will need to provide hope and promise after you name the pain.

- Redeem the most common myths about why people do not pursue radically generous lives. Ideas may include not being able to give at this time, there are too many options, or I do not trust charitable organizations. You may think back through what makes people hesitant at every stage of giving, whether they are a beginner or experienced donor. Break through the deception and affirm direction with spiritual truth. Remember to identify with each type of generous disciple you identified in message two from Exodus 31.

You may consider highlighting some items like the following:

- Discipleship or financial training classes that are offered

- The practices and policies your church has in place to maintain its integrity level on finances

- The different ways members can give financially, such as online, automatic bank drafts, or via text or an app

- Encourage and challenge the congregation to pray for upcoming generosity opportunities

Message #4: *Exodus 33-34 "The Second Chance"*

Exodus 34 is about positive restoration. They may have missed God's intentional plan the first time, but grace abounds. New opportunities exist every day. The generous life doesn't begin once you get everything fixed, get a raise, or start a new job. The generous life begins today.

I want to point out that this chapter actually describes different ways we can be engaged in generosity moving forward. I hope that these parallel with the different types of givers you previously outlined in message two in this series. Also, you will be able to unpack different types of donations your church is able receive throughout the year thus engaging all types of donors.

Festivals of Unleavened Bread and Weeks (34:18, 22)

These are yearly festivals celebrated in the spring and early summer remembering the deliverance by God of the Israelites from Egypt and the deliverance by God of the Law to the Israelites. This is an offering that is solely about the character and activity of God. Giving is a reminder of all that God has delivered us from and called us to. His mighty acts and extension of a relationship are the only reasons we need to be generous toward Him.

Ingathering (34:22)

The ingathering was held in early fall at a time of the year when the crops were harvested. The celebration was marked by living in booths or tents. This was a sign of their former temporary homes and dependence upon God. The festival was uniquely marked by a time of great feasting. This could provide a parallel to periodic offerings your church conducts for special needs like benevolence, youth camps, mission trips, etc. The idea of celebrating and feasting is a powerful twist on how we should commonly express generosity.

First Fruits (34:19, 26)

This type of offering is repeated throughout scripture. We are called to bring God our first and our best. This can speak to disciplined, prioritized, and percentage giving that your church accepts on a regular basis. The first fruits offering is an expression of faith acknowledging who is the owner and provider of our lives. It is a weekly reminder and grounding for all believers.

Not Coming Empty Handed (34:20)

Generosity is for everyone. We should always be ready, prepared, and willing. God expected everyone to participate in the offerings. It had nothing to do with their level of income. It was a sign of a faithful way of life. The term "empty handed" is also used to refer to how we send people away. We are encouraged to not send people away from us empty handed. It has a relational benevolence call. This is a daily offering of our lives and resources to the needs around us.

I love the insiders look at the discipline of prayer and fasting. This passage powerfully gives a living testimony of Moses seeking God in the Tent of Meeting. Below are some of the reasons why prayer and fasting are critical to the generous life.

- It releases our dependence upon the physical for a season

- It focuses our attention on God

- It increases our ability to hear God

- It helps us become more sensitive to what God is doing around us and in others

- It increases our faith

You may consider highlighting some items like the following:

- Upcoming generosity opportunities that match with a positive growth step of each type of giver

- A commitment card that helps them identify the type of giver they are and a commitment to take growth steps over the next 12 months

- A guide to prayer and fasting

Message #5: *Exodus 35:1-29 "Willingness"*

This message is about willingness (35:5). I would consider setting it up to have a large and visionary feel regarding the work of God through your church. You may take the opportunity to share about God's amazing work through your church in the past year. You could provide testimonies, an inspirational video, and even a full color documented Annual Report. This is a great time to help people fall in love with their church and gain a new appreciation and trust. You can show them where both dollars and volunteers are invested with an eternal result.

I would then dream about the next year. What are three specific initiatives you feel God is calling you to accomplish? Several of these initiatives could have a special generosity component. You may want to look back over the week four *Staff Team Up* exercise.

Scripture follows this pattern: The vision is shared (4-19), the people withdraw to seek God (20), the people willingly surrendered, and everyone had a role to play (22-29).

I would conclude the message with a season of prayer and fasting over their commitment cards. In the following weeks ahead you can have them declare the type of giver they are and their willingness to grow. They can also participate immediately in one of the generosity opportunities you have shared.

Message #6: *Exodus 35:30-36:7 "Extraordinary Generosity"*

It is important to talk about the rewards of obedience. Too much emphasis is on the pain and sacrifice of giving. When we give, we are doing the right thing and that should be a blessing. In this story, the same characters return from Exodus 31. Only this time everyone fulfills God's plan.

Here are some directions you may go:

- God places the resources in your hands for a reason. Everything He needed to complete the project was in the hands of His people. They had also previously failed in Exodus 32, yet still had more than enough resources to fulfill obedience.

- God wants you to live generous lives in your careers. Bazalel and Oholiab took their trade and surrendered it. How can you live the generous life beyond the church offering? What does a marketplace faith look like?

- When God provides and you give, He will continue to give so that you can be more generous. The people gave repeatedly.

- God's plan for us together is bigger than His plan for you alone.

- Our lives are not primarily for our benefit or enjoyment, but for an eternal investment for His glory.

Here are some of the positive effects of giving you learned from your study in Proverbs. These can be used to support your message or even define your message.

- **Proverbs 2:7** - He holds success in His hand.

- **Proverbs 3:9-10** - Honor the Lord with your wealth and He will overflow it.

- **Proverbs 8:18** - God possesses riches, wealth, and honor.

- **Proverbs 10:3** - The Lord does not allow the righteous to go hungry.

- **Proverbs 11:10-11** - The city is blessed by the righteous.

- **Proverbs 12:11, 14:23** - God promises abundant food and profit to those who work hard.

- **Proverbs 18:10-11** - God promises to be our protector and provider, not our wealth.

- **Proverbs 19:17** - Giving to the poor is seen as giving to God and will be rewarded.

- **Proverbs 21:1** - God can move the hearts of others to bless His people.

- **Proverbs 23:18** - A promised future hope exists for those who follow God's wisdom.

I would close the service with an offering participation and commitment time. The commitment can have them embrace the type of giver they are and their willingness to grow over the next 12 months. Then have them immediately participate in an offering of some type.

ABOUT THE AUTHOR

Todd McMichen has served for more than 30 years in a variety of roles in the local church, doing everything from planting churches to lead pastor. Todd's generosity roots arise from three capital campaigns he led for two local churches where he served as a staff member. Those two churches alone raised over $35,000,000. Since 2000, Todd has been a well-established stewardship and generosity campaign coach, as well as a conference leader and speaker. Todd is a graduate of Palm Beach Atlantic College in West Palm Beach, Florida and Southwestern Seminary in Ft. Worth, Texas. He lives in Birmingham, Alabama with his wife Theresa, and their two kids, Riley and Breanna. Visit Todd's blog at toddmcmichen.com or follow on twitter @toddmcmichen.

THE INTENTIONAL LEADER SERIES

The Intentional Leader Series is brought to you by the Auxano Team. We invite you to check out the suite of resources at VisionRoom.com, including:

Practical solutions for church leaders
through book summaries

High-level thinking.
Ground-level application.

---

auxano®

auxano.com | visionroom.com | willmancini.com

Other books in the Intentional Leaders Series:

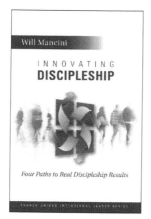

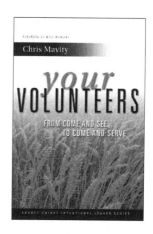

Upcoming Books in the Intentional Leaders Series:

#20s Church
by Heather Stevens and Will Mancini

Question Zero:
What Are We Trying To Accomplish?
by Vince Antonucci

Less Church, More Life:
Why Churches Do Too Much and What To Do About It
by Will Mancini

58509756R00076

Made in the USA
Charleston, SC
12 July 2016